Travel to Tokyo

Where to eat, stay, and play.

SUZANNE LOWE

Silvergum Publishing

AUSTRALIA

First Published in 2024 Silvergum Publishing
www.silvergumpublishing.com

Design by Silvergum Publishing

National Library of Australia Cataloguing-in-Publication entry
Lowe, Suzanne, author.
978-0-6-48904984 (paperback)
978-0-6-48904977 (eBook)
Subject, Travel, Asia, Japan

Thank you to my family, Steve, Tahlia and Emilie, my travelling companions.
A special thanks to Tahlia for translating for us and all the times we asked her, "What does this say?" and "Are we on the right train?!" You made our Japan adventures a lot easier!

Foreword

How to have a stress-free holiday

So, you want to take a holiday to Japan; however, you're not sure where to begin? What do you pack? Will you like the food? How will you get around? Well, you are not alone in asking these questions and *Travel to Tokyo* is here to help you.

I took my first trip overseas to New Zealand with my family when I was twelve years old and from that moment on, the travel bug bit. As I grew into adulthood, I began to travel regularly, learning through many experiences both good and bad, what to pack, when to book and what generally makes a trip overseas less stressful. Because who wants a holiday to be stressful, right? Holidays are your time to enjoy yourself. Whether it be lazing on the beach, looking at museums and temples, or ziplining down a mountain, an enjoyable holiday needs some thought and planning.

There will always be times when things go wrong on holiday, and sometimes these things, like bad weather or lost luggage, are out of your control. Most times, you can prevent disaster by being organised. If you follow a few simple guidelines, then the chances of your trip being a whole lot less stressful are increased.

The tips and guidelines I provide in this book are there for you to use during and before your holiday to Japan, to help make your trip easier. They are derived from my own experiences as a traveller. I have been to Japan on holiday many times with my family, and although sometimes challenging, Japan remains one of my favourite places to visit, and yes, I would definitely go back again!

Look out for the handy **TIPS** throughout the book. They are my own personal hints to make your trip to Japan fun.

My first trip to Japan in 2006 was quite challenging as no one in our family spoke any Japanese and minimal tourist facilities were available at that time. However, travel in Japan in recent years has become much easier. Many signs are now in English, WI-FI is available, and although the language barrier can still be difficult, you can use a translator app on your phone such as Google translator to translate menus, signs etc.

Travel in Japan is great fun and a lot easier than you might think. So, if you are thinking of taking a holiday to Japan, go ahead and do it, you will love it!

Oki o tskukete! (Safe travels!)

Disclaimer:

Japan is changing all the time with some restaurants or attractions closing and new ones opening. Prices may increase, and new trends emerge.
I have based this book on my own personal experiences of the times I have visited Japan with my own family. Some of the information provided may become outdated, and I will revise as I become aware of any changes, for example, admission costs or opening hours. Please take the time to check opening and closing times, prices, addresses etc. yourselves on the websites I have provided to confirm information.

Australian spelling and the metric system are used throughout this book.

If you have any constructive feedback, suggestions or would like to ask me about my family trips to Japan or any other places I have travelled, please contact me through my website
www.suzanneloweauthor.com
I would love to hear from you.
Suzanne

Contents

• CHAPTER 1 •

Why travel to Japan?

I found Japan to be an amazing travel destination. A beguiling mixture of old and modern, futuristic cities and traditional temples all rolled into one. There is always something interesting and quirky to see, whether it be Geishas wandering the streets of Kyoto in traditional kimonos, futuristic robots in Tokyo's National Museum of Emerging Science or eating rainbow-coloured toasted sandwiches in Harajuku.

We always felt safe when travelling in Japan. The people are tremendously polite, and the transport system is extremely efficient, making it easy to get around. I once left my handbag sitting on a seat in a subway train whilst travelling to Shinjuku, and a local Japanese lady exited the train and hurriedly ran after us to ensure I didn't lose it.

Another aspect of Japan that we found gratifying was the customer service ethic. Customers are always treated in high regard, and every effort is made to ensure your happiness. We were always made to feel welcome. On our first trip to Japan when our children were younger, we sat down at a restaurant to eat an evening meal. We suddenly realised that the restaurant only had chopsticks available, no knives and forks and were wondering how the children would eat. Suddenly, we saw one of the restaurant's waiters running down the street, returning a few moments later with a set of knives and forks he had purchased from a nearby convenience store! We hadn't asked for the cutlery; however, he could see we would probably need it. We felt a little embarrassed but also grateful as customers.

If you enjoy photography and posting on social media sites, Tokyo is a wonderful place to snap some interesting photos. From the cute food and toys, amazing science and technology, beautiful temples, and gardens, and quirky nick-nacks, you will find something interesting to photograph. I have many "remember when" moments from Japan and lots of fun stories.

If you are looking for a safe place to go on holiday that can provide some culture, history, innovativeness, and fun then Tokyo is an amazing place to visit.

Japan at a glance

Climate

I have been to Japan in the winter, spring and autumn, and each season has been completely different. My eldest daughter has travelled to Japan in summer, and the humidity can be extremely challenging!

December–February is winter and is generally cold and mostly dry. This is a great time for ski-ing and to see the many Christmas light displays around the major cities. There is also the Sapporo snow festival held in February with ice sculptures and ice slides. Temperatures range from 12 degrees C (54 degrees F) to -1 degrees C (30 degrees F). Temperatures in the mountains can be colder.

March–May is spring and a wonderful time to see displays of cherry blossoms. Golden week (May) also falls during this time. The temperature in spring is a milder 13 degrees C (55 degrees F) to 26 degrees C (79 degrees F).

June–August is summer and can be hot and humid. This is the rainy season for Japan. Temperatures range from 31 degrees C (88 F) to 21 degrees C (70 F). Summer is a good time to visit

Hokkaido and Okinawa as they receive less rain. Typhoons can occur in August.

September–November is autumn and a wonderful time to see the reds and oranges of the autumn leaves. Typhoons can occur in September and the temperatures remain hot and humid. By October the weather is warm; however, no longer humid. Temperatures range from 8 degrees C (46 degrees F) to 28 degrees C (82 degrees F).

Language

The official language is Japanese with the three different writing systems of Kanji, Hiragana, and Katakana. While we found that most people in the cities such as Tokyo and Osaka spoke English, once we headed out into the countryside and smaller towns, communication became more difficult. The Japanese people were always very friendly; however, a phrasebook was extremely useful. For several handy phrases, see the section on *Useful phrases* in the rear of this book.

Religion

The main religions are Shintoism and Buddhism. The Torii, bright red vermillion painted wood gates marking the entrance to a shrine, are the most recognisable icons of Shinto. We saw amazing displays of Torii at Inari Fushimi near Osaka, where hundreds of the red gates lined the mountainside. Good luck charms called omamori are often for sale at Shinto shrines.

Most pagodas and temples in Japan, such as the Senso-Ji Temple in Tokyo are Buddhist places of worship. The Kinkaku-Ji or Golden Temple in Kyoto is a famous Buddhist temple covered entirely in gold leaf.

Geography

The country of Japan is situated in Eastern Asia between the Sea of Japan and the North Pacific Ocean. Japan is made up of four major islands which are Hokkaido in the north, Honshu, the main central island, Kyushu, and Shikoku. There are also several other smaller islands including Okinawa in the south.

Time

Japan runs on a single time zone which is very useful. There is no daylight saving. The time zone is 9 hours ahead of Greenwich Mean time, 14 hours ahead of Eastern Standard time and 17 hours ahead of Pacific standard time. In Australia, Japan is one hour ahead of Western Australia, half an hour behind Southern Australia and one hour behind Eastern Australia.

What to pack

So, what should you take with you? On our first trip to Japan, I packed way too many items and trying to coax several overloaded suitcases up the numerous steps of Tokyo Station in the middle of peak hour (which is something to behold!) was like watching an oxygen deprived climber stagger up mount Everest!

To make your holiday a little less strenuous, these are my suggestions for what to pack when travelling in Japan. It does depend on the time of year you are going and what you will be doing, for example in winter it can get very cold, so you are going to need to bring warm jackets, however, these suggestions will give you some idea on what we packed the second time we travelled!

<u>Wear good socks!</u> You will be taking your shoes off a lot, for example, when you are visiting temples, some restaurants and if staying in a Ryokan (Japanese Inn). You don't want to have socks with holes in them. It's not a good look!

<u>Pack light.</u> You will probably be doing a lot of walking, using public transport, and moving between places. Lugging heavy baggage when you are tired or trying to find your hotel is not a happy situation, especially when you must navigate busy train stations bursting with commuters or carry your belongings up

large flights of stairs. Most subways and some train stations, especially those in smaller towns, do not have elevators for public use.

Bring comfortable walking shoes. You will be walking a lot! Some places, such as gaming centres require closed-in shoes for safety reasons.

Wear shoes you can take on and off easily. If you are travelling with children, use Velcro shoes or slip ons. It is not always easy to remove and replace your shoes perched on the steps of a temple or restaurant, so you want to make this as easy as possible, especially for younger children or if you have mobility difficulties.

Bring a light jacket or wrap even in summer as the department stores, trains and hotels have their air-conditioning on high, and I often found myself getting cold when shopping. However, because the temperature outside is warm, you will find yourself constantly putting your jacket on and taking it off so bring something light and easy to carry.

Pack casual, neat clothing that doesn't require ironing, such as jeans, skirts, t-shirts or tops, light dresses. Again, it depends upon the time of year you will be visiting. When we went in winter, we also brought boots and a light rain jacket. Umbrellas are easily purchased from the many convenience stores around the city.

Bring any medication you require with you as it may not be available and trying to explain what you want may be difficult.

Think compact. We used either a small day bag or handbag with wide comfortable straps to carry around during the day. Something medium-sized without being too cumbersome.

Bring charging cords for electronics. For example, cameras, iPads, phones etc. may need different charging chords. Bring these with you, plus several adapters. Japan uses 100 volts, 50 Hz. (See the section on electricity, for more information). I always pack these together in a separate small packing cell or zip lock bag and carry them in my hand luggage on the plane just in case my luggage goes missing or I want to charge something at the airport. Spare batteries need to be carried in your hand luggage when flying.

Many cafes have power points available to charge your phone; however, they are obviously for Japanese plugs so you will need to carry an adapter if you want to use them.

Travel utensils. If you are travelling with children or find it difficult to use chopsticks, a useful item is a small knife and fork set. Most restaurants only supply chopsticks so these can be very handy. Don't pack them in your carry-on baggage when flying or you will be asked to leave them behind! This also applies to domestic air travel.

Bring a photocopy of your passport. Don't forget your passports for everyone in your group, plus any credit card or travel cards you are taking. I always make a copy of my passport to leave with a family member or friend at home in case mine is lost or stolen when travelling.

Arriving in Tokyo

Narita International Airport

The Narita international airport in Tokyo has two terminals which are connected by a free shuttle bus.
The tourist information offices are located in the arrival lobby of both terminals. https://www.narita-airport.jp/en/service/

To journey into central Tokyo, you can:

- Use a taxi which will be expensive, usually around 22 000 yen or more during peak times.
- Catch the airport limousine bus approx. 1 hour or more during peak hours. www.okkbus.co.jp
- Catch a Keisei Skyliner train approx. 50 minutes, seats are reserved (located beneath the terminal building).
- Catch the Narita Express (NEX) train also located beneath the terminal building. Approx. 50 minutes. The Japan Rail Pass can be used on this line, and seats need to be reserved at the ticket booth.

Find more information see the airport website. https://www.narita-airport.jp/en/access/city_access

Kansai International Airport (KIX)

Osaka is the third-largest city in Japan and is located in the Kansai region of Honshu, the largest of the islands that make up Japan. Kansai International Airport handles flights from around the world including Australia, UK, Europe, and America.
The tourist information centre is located in the arrival hall. https://www.kansai-airport.or.jp/en/touristinfo/

To journey into Osaka or Kyoto from the airport, you can:

- Catch an airport limousine bus (www.okkbus.co.jp) to Osaka Station (25 minutes), Namba Station (35 minutes) and Shin-Osaka Station (25 minutes). Tickets can be purchased from the ticket machine located outside the arrival hall.
- Use a Taxi, though often expensive, especially in peak hour traffic.
- Travel by train.

Luggage delivery

If you don't want the hassle of taking your luggage on the train or bus with you and are not in a rush for your luggage, you can use a luggage delivery service. Luggage can be delivered from the airport to your hotel or a private residence the next day. There are service counters for companies offering this service at both Narita and Kansai airports. Luggage can also be picked up from your hotel and delivered to the airport for your return journey.

Getting around easily

The easiest way to travel around the cites in Japan is by train and subway; however, taxis are also easily available.

Taxi

TIPS

If travelling by taxi, there are a couple of things to bear in mind.

Taxis can be expensive so try not to use them in peak hour traffic.

Most taxis do not offer child or baby seats/carriers.

The driver may not speak English or be able to understand you so take a card from your accommodation with the address written in Japanese with you. It makes explaining where you want to go easier.

If you ask the reception at your hotel to write down the name of where you want to go in Japanese (e.g. to a restaurant, temple or park) you can show this to your driver for an easier explanation.

Subway and Train lines

One thing we were surprised about in Japan was how extremely efficient and clean the train and subway lines were. We never saw any rubbish or graffiti anywhere and the trains run almost exactly on time. If a train states it is coming at 5 minutes past 3 o'clock then it will arrive at exactly that time. Don't be late as the train won't wait for you!

On buses, trains and subway, children under 6-years old travel free, while children aged 6-11 travel at half fare.

TIPS

Avoid peak hour at all costs especially when travelling with younger children. The weekday rush hours peak between 8 am and 9 am in the morning, and shortly after 5 pm in the evening. The number of people using the Stations, queuing, and boarding the trains is astounding, and unless you know what you are doing, it can be quite confronting and confusing.

Because peak hour can get so busy with many people waiting to catch a train, the Stations actually employ people called oshiya (you will see them dressed in white gloves) to push/herd people onto the trains in rush hour to squeeze as many people into the carriages as possible.

The trains become very crowded with people crammed up against one another, unable to move, which I found to be very claustrophobic.

Be aware that many stations have a lot of stairs and don't always have elevators or escalators.

Which train to catch?

We often used Google Maps on our mobile phone to figure out which station to use and which trains to catch while we were in both Tokyo and Osaka.

To do this, we simply opened the Google Maps App, typed in our starting address and where we wanted to get to. For example, Asakusa to Shinjuku. Hit enter, then when the results came up, we selected the train icon (or foot if you wanted to walk) and the correct train line to catch would be displayed indicated by colour coding.

Another site we found useful was HyperDia for train timetables and routes. **http://www.hyperdia.com/en/**

Map of Tokyo Subway:

https://www.tokyometro.jp/en/subwaymap/

Map of Jr Trainline:

https://cdn.jrailpass.com/img/public/pdf/JRP_japan.pdf

Map of Shinkansen Trainline:

https://cdn.jrailpass.com/img/public/pdf/Shinkansen-map-jr-pass.pdf

IC cards

IC cards such as Suica, Pasmo and Icoca are rechargeable cards that can be used to conveniently pay fares on local trains, subway, and buses. The correct amount for your fare will be taken from your card as you pass through the ticket gate, which means you don't have to work out the correct fare to pay or carry the right amount of cash. (See the section below on how to use the cards). The cards can also be used to make purchases in many shops and restaurants, making them very convenient.

TIPS

Always place your IC card in an easily accessible place when you are travelling on the train so you know where it is and can locate it quickly. Standing in a very busy crowd of people waiting to depart or enter the train station while you dig around in your bag for your card is not fun!

If you lose your IC card, see the attendants at the ticket counter of the train station. My daughter lost her IC card when we were last in Tokyo, having only used it once, so it was fully loaded. Obviously, I was not very happy; however, the attendants at the ticket counter in Tokyo Station were able to issue her with a new card and the remaining balance without any problem.

How to use IC cards?

As you pass through the automatic ticket gates, touch your IC card onto the card reader for about one second (rather than inserting it into the ticket slot). The applicable fare will automatically be deducted when you exit through the ticket gate at your destination station. When riding on buses, the card readers are positioned at the entrance and/or exit of the bus. A card cannot be shared by multiple travellers at the same time.

Where to get an IC card?

IC cards can be purchased at ticket machines and ticket counters at railway stations. The initial cost consists of a refundable deposit of 500-yen plus an initial amount (typically 1500-yen) to be charged onto the card.

How to recharge IC cards?

IC cards can be recharged at ticket machines and special recharging machines found at railway stations. The maximum amount that can be loaded onto an IC card is 20,000 yen.

How to check the current balance?

The current credit balance of your IC card is shown on the small display whenever you pass a ticket gate or make a payment at a store. You can also check the balance at ticket machines in the train stations.

How to get back the 500-yen refundable deposit?

To get the initial 500-yen deposit made when you first purchased your card refunded, take your card to an attendant at the ticket counter in the train station. You must do this in the city where you initially purchased the card. For example, an IC card purchased in Tokyo can only be refunded in Tokyo not Osaka and vice versa. Unused credit can also be refunded less a handling fee.

Automated ticket gates at train station

Travelling on the Shinkansen (Bullet Train)

Japan's main islands of Honshu, Kyushu and Hokkaido are served by a network of high-speed train lines that connect Tokyo with most of the country's major cities. The high-speed trains or bullet trains called Shinkansen run at speeds of up to 320 km/h and are operated by Japan Railways (JR).

We have always found the bullet trains to be extremely punctual, clean, comfortable (all the seats face forward) and quiet. There are two types of class seats available, ordinary, and green. The green class seats are larger and less crowded.

Wi-Fi is available, and some Shinkansen trains serve snacks, boxed meals (bento boxes) and drinks from small food carts. Others have vending machines available. Toilets are provided on the trains.

Do you need to reserve seats?

Seat reservations allow you to secure a seat and travel with peace of mind, especially if you are travelling in a group or with children and want to sit together. Some train lines get booked out during busy periods such as golden week, school holidays or the weekend. Reservations can be made for all Shinkansen trains but are not mandatory on the trains that also carry non-reserved seating. A fee of a few hundred yen applies for making seat reservations. Japan Rail Pass holders can make seat reservations for free.

Buying a ticket at the ticket counter

Shinkansen tickets can be purchased at any JR ticket office found at JR train stations throughout the country. Foreign Credit Cards are accepted at most ticket offices. To purchase a ticket, you will require the following information:

- Number of people travelling
- Date of travel
- Departure station
- Destination station
- Ordinary or green car
- Reserved or non-reserved seat

For a seat reservation, the following additional information is required:

- Train name (e.g. Hikari) and train number or departure time
- Preference of smoking or non-smoking seat, if available

TIPS

I recommend writing the information on a piece of paper or the note section of your phone and presenting it to the salesperson in order to make the purchasing process smoother. While the staff usually speak some English, it is not always easy to communicate and having information such as the date and number of people travelling written down makes communication easier.

Tickets can also be purchased online or at ticket machines however we found this difficult as most instructions were in Japanese and foreign credit cards were not accepted at the time. For ease, we always used the JR ticket counters to purchase tickets.

Luggage

Each traveller is allowed to bring up to two pieces of luggage onto the train with each piece not weighing more than 30 kilograms and not measuring more than 250 centimetres when adding up width, height, and depth. There is space in the overhead shelves above your seat to place small and medium-sized bags and suitcases. Larger suitcases will need to be placed by your seat.

TIP

If you are travelling with larger suitcases or a stroller/pram, I recommend reserving the last row of seats in the carriage as there is additional space behind these seats for larger items and you won't have to lug your belongings through the aisles of the train.

Shinkansen Bullet Train

How to use the Shinkansen Bullet Train

1) Pass through the regular ticket gate

At many Stations, Shinkansen passengers must pass through two sets of automatic ticket gates, the regular ticket gates and the Shinkansen ticket gates. First, pass through the regular train ticket gate, insert only your base fare ticket into the ticket slot, pass the gate and retrieve your ticket at the other end. Japan Rail Pass holders must show their pass to the staff at the manned gate.

2) Make your way to the Shinkansen platforms

Follow the signs to the Shinkansen platforms which may either be close to the regular train platforms or maybe in a separate part or on a different level. If you are unsure of where to go, ask a Station Assistant located near the ticket gates.

3) Pass through the Shinkansen ticket gates

The second set of gates divides the Shinkansen platforms from the regular train platforms, although at some stations there are also direct gates to the Shinkansen platforms that allow passengers to skip the regular gates. This time insert not only your base fare ticket but also your supplement ticket together into the ticket slot at the same time and retrieve them on the other side of the gate. Japan Rail Pass holders again use the manned gate, instead.

4) Access your platform

Look at the display boards which show the upcoming train departures. The board will state the platform from which your train will depart.

5) Find your carriage

Once you've made your way to the correct platform, find which carriage you will be in. Markings on the platform floor will show where each numbered carriage door will open and whether it is a reserve or green carriage. Line up with the other passengers ready to board the train.

6) Find your seat

Once onboard, find your seat and stow your luggage overhead or by your seat. Don't block the isles. Seats are numbered and lettered in the same style as on airplanes.

Rules for using the Shinkansen include:

Don't block the isles with your luggage.

Set your mobile phone to silent.

Don't talk on your phone except when in the deck areas between carriages.

Line up on the platform before boarding.

Return your seat to the upright position before exiting the train.

JR passes

The Japan Rail Pass (also commonly called JR Pass) is a very cost-effective rail pass for long-distance train travel. The pass can be used by foreign tourists only and offers unlimited use of JR trains for one, two or three weeks. It comes in two types: ordinary and green carriages (first-class carriages).

If you are doing any long-distance travel for example, Tokyo to Osaka or Kyoto, I found the JR rail pass to be very easy to use and a cost saving, although prices have increased in recent years.

Location of places in Japan

Many restaurants and hotels are located either above or below ground level. We once became totally lost looking for our hotel as we didn't realise the hotel reception was located on the twenty-third floor of the building we were looking at. There were offices located on the bottom floors of the building, and the hotel was on top.

Another time we were looking for the Alice in Wonderland restaurant in Tokyo, and it took us quite a while to locate it. Eventually, we found it on the basement level of a shopping complex, down a flight of stairs and tucked away in a corner!

TIPS

Don't expect restaurants, shops, and hotel lobbies to be on the ground level. Always consider they may be several stories above where you are looking, below ground, or hidden away amongst office buildings.

Japan follows the same system of flooring as the USA. For example, when a business/ attraction says it is located on the first floor that means it is on the ground floor for Australians and the English. The second floor means it is on the first floor of the building for Australians and the English.

• CHAPTER 2 •

Eating out

Japan is a wonderful place to try a great variety of foods you may not have at home. The food is generally very well priced, nicely decorated and often very "Kawai" cute!

TIPS on eating out are:
Each restaurant usually specialises in a particular type of food. For example, a sushi restaurant will not sell ramen (noodle broth).

Something to be aware of which we discovered on our first trip to Tokyo is that most restaurants do not have forks. So, unless you are handy with chopsticks, take your own knife and fork set with you when eating out. You can purchase these at supermarkets in a handy carry case before you leave home. Just make sure you pack them in your checked suitcase and not in your carry-on hand luggage.

Many restaurants have plastic displays of the food they offer on display in the window of their eatery, which makes it easier to see what is available.

Fake food displays outside a restaurant

There are many affordable restaurants and eateries located in train Stations (usually on the lower levels) and in food halls in department stores such as the Takashimaya and Daimaru Department stores (located in the basement levels). See the section on shopping for examples of where to find department stores.

Japanese food can be seasonal so, certain foods may only be available at particular times of the year.

Eateries often have a number system where you choose the corresponding number to the food you wish to order, take a ticket from a machine, and pay at the counter. Servers will then bring you your food once it is cooked.
Tipping is not required in Japan.

Nearly every restaurant we went to provided free iced water or tea with our meal, which was very handy.

Vegans may have a difficult time finding food that suits them, as even vegetable dishes use dashi stock made with dried tuna flakes. Ask your hotel concierge to write a note in Japanese saying you are Vegan as it may help to show this to the wait staff at restaurants.

We found that restaurants often have low-price child meals available. If you are travelling with children, ask for the *Oko sama setto* which is a children's set meal, or *Kidozu menyuu,* children's menu.

Savory

These are some of my favourite savory meals I enjoyed in Japan.

Okonomiyaki is a savoury egg and noodle pancake to which a variety of toppings are added including pork, prawn, shrimp, chicken, and vegetables.

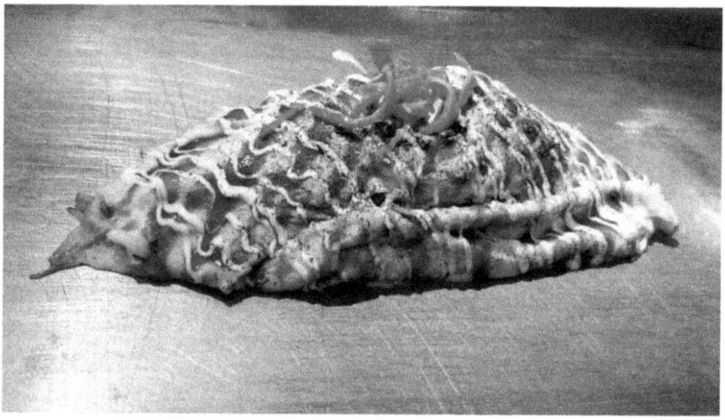

Okonomiyaki

Curry rice Japanese curry is milder and more smooth than other styles of curry. Katsu-kare is a curry served with a breaded pork cutlet and is very popular. Curry rice can be found at Joto Curry.

Yakitori Skewered chicken or other meat typically brushed with a sweet soy sauce glaze and barbecued over coals. Yakitori can be found in Yakitori Street Kabuki-Cho, in Shinjuku.

Nabe is hotpots of meat or seafood with vegetables and noodles. You add the ingredients to a simmering broth yourself and eat when cooked.

Ramen tasty hot noodles served in a rich broth. Additions include corn, boiled egg, pork slices, shallots, bean sprouts, seaweed strips, tofu. *Ichiran Ramen* is a popular ramen chain of restaurants throughout Japan. *Ramen Street* at the basement 1 level of Tokyo Train Station near the Yaesu South Exit is worth visiting. Eight of Tokyo's best ramen restaurants have set up shop and serve excellent Ramen; there is often a queue.

Ramen and Gyoza

Tonkatsu is a little like a schnitzel. A thick pork cutlet breaded and deep-fried to a golden crisp. *Maisen* is a popular tonkatsu restaurant.

Tonkatsu ready to eat

Sushi train Little plates of food circle around on a conveyer belt and you simply choose what you want to eat and pay for the total amount of plates at the end. Nemuro Hanamaru is an example of a conveyor belt sushi restaurant.

Shabu is a hotpot dish of thinly sliced meat, vegetables and noodles boiled in a broth. We loved this dish as you can often cook your own at the restaurant table. An example is *Kisoji* in Tokyo.

Shabu cooking

Gyoza is another of our favourites. Dumplings that are either fried or steamed and include pork, seafood or vegetables accompanied with a dipping sauce. We prefer the fried variety which has a crispy base. *Harajuku Gyozarou* is a popular restaurant serving Gyoza in Tokyo.

Gyoza, hot and ready to eat

Yoshoku is the name given to Western foods that have been uniquely adapted to Japanese tastes through the use of Japanese ingredients and techniques. An example is the *Spaghetti Hashiya* restaurant in Shinjuku, Tokyo, which serves only spaghetti but with Japanese sauces.

Chain Restaurants and Themed Restaurants - If you want a change from Japanese food, there are several restaurant chains which serve western-style food with a Japanese twist. Examples are Starbucks, Hardrock Cafes, Krispy Cremes, Freshness Burger, Denny's, and themed restaurants such as Alice in Wonderland and the Hello Kitty Cafe. ***(See the section on themed cafes for suggestions.)***

Convenience Stores

Convenience stores stock ready-made meals such as bento boxes, onigiri rice balls and ramen noodles. On one of our trips to Japan, we arrived in the evening and after a long flight, everyone was tired. After checking into our hotel rather than finding a restaurant to eat at we went to a Lawson's family mart located next door to where we were staying and bought some ready-made food to take back to the hotel. It was an easy, cheap, and simple solution for dinner. Examples of convenience stores in Tokyo are 7-Eleven, Lawley's, and Family Mart.

Food Halls

The food halls in the major department stores such as the Takashimaya and Daimaru in Japan are amazing and an excellent place to find food to take back to your hotel if you want a break from eating out. They are usually located in the basement floors.

TIP

Even if you are not buying anything, the food halls are a wonderful place to look at. There are so many interesting foods, all brightly wrapped and presented that it's a fun place to browse, especially if the weather turns rainy.

Japanese sweets and desserts

Japanese sweets and desserts are often quite different from western-style desserts in both look and taste. They are generally less sweet but taste just as nice and you don't feel as though you've had a sugar overload.

There are so many cute desserts to choose from and they make great photos too, that it's hard to resist wanting to try them all!

These are a few of my favourites.

Dango

Dango are sweet Japanese dumplings made from rice flour and served on a bamboo stick with a sweet dipping sauce. They can be white or coloured light pink or green.

Mochi

Mochi are similar to Dango and are sweet Japanese rice cakes cooked and moulded into a round shape. They can be plain, filled with a sweet red bean paste (Anko) or filled with a whole strawberry (Ichigo daifuku).

Baked Pablo Cheesecake

This creamy baked cheesecake is another of my favourites. Rich and creamy in texture similar to an egg tart you can find these desserts in the Pablo shop in Akihabara and Shinjuku in Tokyo.

Parfait

Although not Japanese in origin, parfaits are another popular choice of dessert, and they are usually very colourful and filled with fruits.

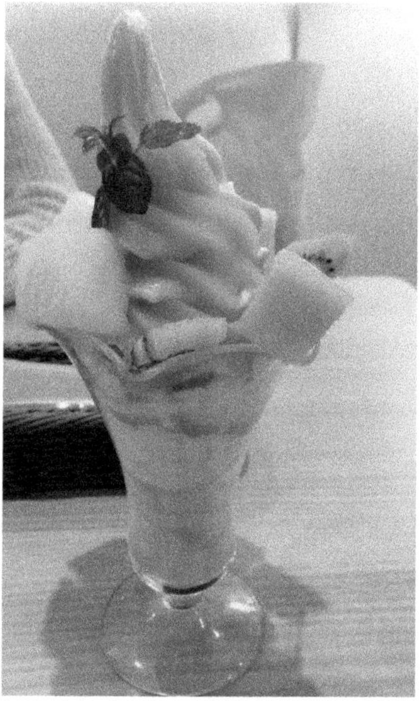

Fruit Parfait.

Taiyaki

Taiyaki are one of my favourite Japanese sweets! These fish-shaped pastries are cooked in a "waffle iron" and filled with Anko (a sweet red bean paste), custard or chocolate. Taiyaki are a cross between a waffle and a pancake and taste delightful.

Crepes

Cream and fruit-filled crepes are very popular, and you will find stores selling them everywhere, particularly in Harajuku. The crepes are wrapped in the style of an ice cream cone and filled with whichever filling you choose, chocolate, custard, cream, and a selection of fruits.

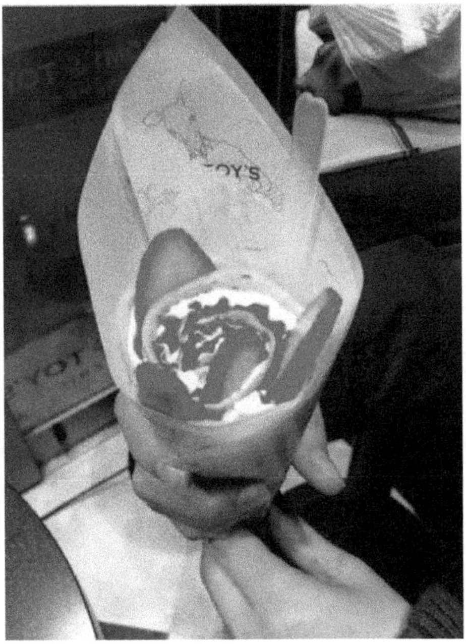

Strawberry and cream crepes

Kakigori (shaved ice)

Kakigori is Japanese shaved ice served with syrup, especially popular during the summer. The ice is shaved in a way that it has a fluffy powder snow like texture different from a snow cone. Kakigori was once a dessert reserved only for the Japanese royal family it is now very popular throughout Japan. The Ice is usually served with a syrup, the most popular flavours being lemon, blue Hawaii, melon, and strawberry.

Kakigori with strawberry syrup

Strawberry Shortcake

The strawberry shortcake adapted from Western culture. Is traditionally eaten in Japan on Christmas Eve. Made of soft layers of sponge cake, fresh strawberries & fresh whipped cream, this cake is a delight!

Strawberry Shortcake

Bakeries

Although not a traditional Japanese food, I just had to mention the bakeries they have in Japan. They serve rows and rows of tempting pastries and bread both savoury and sweet, often decorated as cute characters and animals which my children just adored. They make an easy lunchtime snack too, just be sure not to walk around while eating them as it is considered bad manners to eat and walk. Find a park to sit in or take them back to your hotel.

Chapter Three

Money, Money, Money

The currency in Japan is the Yen ¥. Coins come in 1, 5, 10, 50, 100 and 500-yen. Banknotes are 1000, 2000, 5000 and 10,000-yen. Japan is predominantly a cash-based society; many shops and restaurants, particularly smaller establishments do not accept credit cards. There are many ATMs in Japan; however, many do not accept foreign cards. However, the ATM's at 7-Eleven convenience stores, Family Marts and post offices will accept foreign cards and have instructions in English.

There are currency exchange counters at the international airports usually open from 6.30 am to 11 pm. Banks such as Citibank, Mizuho Bank and Sumitomo Mitsui also exchange foreign currency. You will need your passport for identification. Opening hours for banks are 9 am–3 pm weekdays. Larger hotels may also offer currency exchange.

Gashapon machines

TIPS

Keep your 100-yen coins for the Gashapon (machine dispensed capsule toys) and the huge variety of vending machines available throughout Japan. You will find vending machines in train stations, department stores, in parks and on street corners. You know you are going to want to try them out and they only take coins so keep your 100-yen coins!

I always bring some Japanese yen with me from home before I arrive in Japan. This is especially useful if you want to catch a taxi from the airport or if you need to buy water or food. Also, if you arrive on the weekend or after hours when banks will be closed, already having a small amount of cash with you is handy.

Another tip is to use a travel cash card (usually obtained from your bank or a currency conversion service before you leave home). You can load money in Japanese yen onto the card before you leave home and use it to withdraw money at ATMs in post offices or family marts once in the country.

Other options are digital travel cards such as Wise where you load currency directly to your mobile phone from your bank account onto an app which can then be used to pay for items.

Japanese electronic travel cards such as those used for train and bus travel like the Suica Card or Pasmo Card can also be loaded with cash at train stations. These cards are reloadable and are often accepted at convenience stores for purchasing products and vending machines. Note that as they are a local card, only Japanese Yen can be loaded onto the card.

Tipping is not required in Japan.

If you are planning on using a credit or debit card while overseas, remember to inform your bank before you leave home. Let them know you will be making purchases overseas, the countries you will be travelling to and the dates you will be travelling. Otherwise, your bank may suspect fraudulent activity and suspend your account leaving you without a credit card! I've had it happen while on holiday and it's a shock and huge inconvenience.

Chapter Four

Where to stay

You will probably get a shock when you first enter your hotel room in Japan as the rooms are generally very small compared to many hotels in western countries, and their bathrooms are compact. A few hotels will offer "larger family rooms" which may be corner rooms that provide more bedding such as triple single beds.

What to consider

When you are deciding on which hotel to book, there are several things to consider.

Is the hotel near transport? If you are not hiring a car and plan on travelling around, even if it is only locally, you will need easy access to transport. Trains, buses, trams, or the subway should be located within walking distance.

Is the hotel near restaurants and entertainment? You may or may not wish to be in the centre of things.

If your hotel is out of town, is there transport nearby?

Are transfers from the airport to your hotel included or available to book? Or will you need to organise your own way of getting to the hotel when you arrive?

Is breakfast included, or is it at an extra charge?

Is Wi-Fi free?

Do they have a pool or gym available? Do you have to pay extra to use it? Some hotels, especially Ryokans (Inns) have hot tubs/springs available for use.

When booking your room, you may want to specify that you would like:

Smoking or non-smoking.

Twin or double room for bed configuration.

Do you want to be close or further away from the elevators?

Do you want to be on a higher or lower floor? Some older style/ smaller hotels/Pensions may only have stairs available. This can be important if your hotel does not have an elevator and you have a stroller or a lot of luggage.

Can you request an early check-in or late check-out if required? Or if this is not possible, are you able to leave your luggage in a secure location at the hotel? If for example, you have a late flight and do not wish to drag your luggage around with you while you wait to go to the airport/train station.

TIPS

A lot of hotels offer free upgrades, priority check-in, free Wi-Fi, or other bonuses if you are a member of that particular chain of hotel. It may be worthwhile joining up, especially if you are planning on staying in one of their hotels, again.

If you are staying overseas for a longer period of time, particularly with children, or with a larger group, it may be worthwhile staying in an apartment rather than a hotel room. This way you don't have to book several rooms which can get expensive, and you can spread out a lot more. Most apartments come with parking spaces too, which can be handy if you are renting a car. The downside is that there is usually not a restaurant on site. However, if you book an apartment that is close to cafes, restaurants, pubs etc. or transport so that you can get to restaurants, this is not usually a problem. An apartment also usually comes with a small kitchen and a laundry, which is very handy for longer stays and easy breakfasts!

A great tip when staying in Japan is to take one of the hotel's business cards with you when you are out and about. The card will have the hotel's address and phone number written in Japanese and is very useful for showing taxi drivers and train Station attendants when trying to explain where you want to go. Not everyone speaks English, and even fewer people read English, so trying to explain where you want to go using an English map can be a challenge.

Examples of areas to stay in Tokyo.

The best neighbourhood to stay in Tokyo will depend upon your budget, and how much you intend to travel around the city. You may want to stay close to Tokyo Station so you can get around easily, or you may want to stay close to the theme parks if you intend to spend a few days visiting them.

TIPS You don't have to stay in the same hotel for your entire stay. When we visited Tokyo on our last holiday, we first stayed

in Shinjuku so we could be close to the shopping areas, then, for the last couple of days we stayed at a hotel close to Disney Land and Disney Sea as we intended on getting to the parks early to beat the crowds.
Try to book a hotel that is close to the Yamanote line as this is the most useful train line for visiting the main tourist sites in Tokyo.

Shinjuku

This neighbourhood is full of bright neon lights, bustling streets, and tall buildings with billboards like the Japan you see in movies. Shinjuku is a main transport hub and is on the Yamanote train line making it easy to get to everywhere from here. There are loads of restaurants and shopping areas.

Shibuya

Similar to Shinjuku, Shibuya is also a great place to stay for shopping and eating. There are easy transport options and a youthful feeling to this area. The famous Shibuya crossing is in this area.

Tokyo Bay

Tokyo Bay is popular with travellers wanting to stay near the theme parks. A lot of the hotels in this area cater well to families. The downside is that this area is further away from the main city area and travel downtown can take half an hour to an hour depending on where you need to go.

Asakusa

This neighbourhood is one of the older areas of Tokyo so the hotels here can be cheaper making it ideal if you are on a budget. Many of the hotels in this area have larger rooms with triple and quad bedding, making them ideal for larger groups of travellers. The Senso-ji temple and markets are also in this area.

Maranouchi/Tokyo Station

Tokyo station is the biggest transport hub in Tokyo making it a good place to stay if you intend to travel to or from other parts of Japan. There is easy access to the theme parks from this area and a large array of restaurants to choose from. Many sites such as the Imperial palace and park, and the upmarket shopping area of Ginza, are within walking distance from Maranouchi/Tokyo Station.

Examples of hotels in Tokyo

Karaksa Hotel Colours Nihonbashi

This lovely hotel features many different room types perfect for couples, families and groups.

Free wifi throughout

Laundry room for guests

Lounge area and café with snacks and drinks available.

Parcel delivery service

Luggage storage

Sotetsu Fresa Inn

This mid-range hotel is close to the Toyocho train station and has double, triple and quad rooms perfect for travellers travelling in a group.

Free Wi-Fi

Small restaurant available onsite

Coin operated guest laundry and vending machines.

Hotel Mystays Asakusa

This budget hotel has small rooms; however, they are clean and bright and have a kitchenette including a microwave which is very useful. Triple rooms are available, and the hotel is an easy walk to the Senso-ji temple and markets.

Free Wi-Fi

Coin operated guest laundry.
Bicycles available to rent.
Note there is no housekeeping at this hotel.

Nikko Tokyo Daiba

A little out of the main area of Tokyo, this mid-range hotel is however, a great option if you want to stay close to the Disney theme parks. The rooms are larger than usual and there is a family suite available. The hotel is close to the train station and there is a shopping mall close by. The hotel also offers a free shuttle service to the Disneyland theme park.
Free Wi-Fi
Restaurant and convenience store available onsite

Ryokan Kamogawa Tokyo

This traditional ryokan or Japanese guest house is a great way to experience Japanese culture. You sleep on the floor on futon mattresses, meals are served at low tables whilst you are seated on the floor on tatami floor matting and there is an onsite Onsen (bathhouse) to soak in after a long day of sightseeing!
Free Wi-Fi
Restaurant available onsite
The Onsen can be booked privately.
You can choose a western or Japanese breakfast.

Hilton Tokyo Bay

This high-end hotel is Disney's official hotel in Tokyo and has a lot of cute touches such as fairy tailed themed rooms with interactive features. This is a good choice of hotel if you want to visit Disneyland and/or Disney Sea. Triple rooms are available.
Free Wi-Fi and DVD player
Restaurant and deli available onsite
Outdoor and indoor pools for guests
30 minutes from downtown Tokyo

Four Seasons Marunouchi

If you like trains this is the hotel for you! This luxury hotel is located next to the Tokyo station so you can get a great view of the trains coming and going.
Free Wi-Fi
Restaurant available onsite

Hotel Axa Nihonbashi

This friendly hotel has apartment style rooms with a kitchenette and washer/dryer making then ideal for washing your clothes halfway through your holiday! The hotel is only a 5-minute walk from the airport shuttle bus terminal and has a supermarket close by.
Free Wi-Fi
Apple Tv and Netflix available, not a lot of restaurants close by.

Oakwood Premier Apartments

One, two, and three-bedroom apartments with a full kitchen plus washer/dryer are available at this hotel. The hotel is very central with Tokyo station only a 5-minute walk away. The airport shuttle service is also located across the road.

Wi-Fi is only free in the hotel lobby. Paid available in rooms.

Convenience store located on the ground floor.

Takashimaya Department store is located close by

Quirky Hotels in Tokyo

If you are looking for somewhere a little different to stay whilst holidaying in Japan, Tokyo has some quirky hotels that might interest you.

Futuristic hotel

Hann na Hotel
This hotel is located in the Nishikasai neighbourhood of Tokyo Bay. When you arrive at the hotel and enter the hotel lobby you will be checked in by either a slightly scary looking dinosaur (I'm not sure why a dinosaur!) or a female android with blinking eyes. Once checked in your luggage is taken to your room by an automated trolley. Even crazier the hotel has facial recognition technology, so instead of a standard electronic room key, a digital image of your face is registered at the front desk when you check in and used to open your room!
There are robots to clean the rooms and a robot concierge named Unibot offering helpful tips about exploring Tokyo. Triple bedrooms plus a sofa bed are available.
Future plans for the hotel include robot room service and robot entertainment!
Maihama train station is nearby.
Complimentary shuttle service to nearby Tokyo Disneyland and Disneysea

Free Wi-Fi
Non-smoking rooms available
Restaurant onsite

Godzilla themed hotel

Hotel Gracery
Located in Shinjuku, this quirky Tokyo hotel is anything but dull. If you like the uniquely Japanese character Godzilla, then you will love this hotel. From the moment you walk into the lobby you'll be surrounded by all things Godzilla. There are movie posters, scenes, and memorabilia from the Godzilla films. And on the eighth floor, there is an imposing Godzilla head on display which roars at 6pm and 8pm each day. There is also a large Godzilla statue on the roof of the hotel which puts on a show giving an ear-splitting roar and blowing fire, (well smoke) out of his mouth each hour. The hotel also has an interactive Godzilla room and Godzilla-themed treats to commemorate your stay.

You can choose to wake up to the sight of a giant reptilian eyeball peering into your bedroom in the Godzilla view room which looks out directly onto the replica of the movie monster. Or sleep alongside a man-sized Godzilla statue on a bed that is shadowed by an enormous hand. "Normal rooms" are also available, including triple bedrooms. A handy convenience store is located next door.

Close to Shinjuku train station and the Shinjuku Gyoen National Garden
Free Wi-Fi
Restaurant onsite
An information corner with free-use computers, a currency exchange machine, and an ATM machine.
Non-smoking rooms available
Bath available

Anime themed hotel

Keiko Plaza Hotel

Located in the trendy area of Shinjuku, the Keiko Plaza hotel has uniformed bellhops to greet you at the door, kimono clad musicians playing in the lobby, a karaoke parlour on the 47th floor and four Hello Kitty and her friends themed rooms to stay in. In the Hello Kitty room, the cute Sanrio character anime cat is printed on the walls and furniture, there is a giant Hello Kitty plushy in the room and all the amenities and toiletries such as toothbrushes and water bottles are Hello Kitty themed. There is also a green butterfly and rainbow filled My Melody room which pays homage to Hello Kitty's best friend and a Little Twin Stars room for Kiki and Layla with a unicorn above the bed and fairy-tale feel. The hotel also has themed mocktails and breakfast to match the characters.

Located close to the Shinjuku train station. The hotel provides a free shuttle bus to the Tokyo Disney Resort,

Free Wi-Fi
Rooftop swimming pool
Convenience store onsite
Restaurants on site
Non-smoking rooms

Other Character Hotels

Imperial Hotel's Snoopy Room

If you are more of a dog person than Hello Kitty person, then head to the Imperial hotel in Ginza to stay in one of their Peanuts character Snoopy rooms. The Snoopy themed rooms are dotted with everything Snoopy, from cushions, rugs, slippers and robes, cups and plushie toys. There is also a limited-edition Grand Chef Snoopy package available which includes a themed breakfast bento box with take home bag. If you want more to take home, the hotel sells Doorman Snoopy plushies in their gift store.
There is an indoor pool at this hotel including a children's pool. The Park hotel is close to the Imperial Palace.

Free Wi-Fi
Restaurant on site
Bathtubs in room
Non-smoking rooms
Airport shuttle service

Highland Resort and Hotel Thomas the Tank Engine Room

If you are after cuteness, you can book a room at the Highland Resort Hotel located in the Fuji Q Highland Amusement Park at the foot of Mount Fuji. The Thomas and Percy themed rooms are family sized and have detailed murals of Thomas and his friends on the walls. The rooms also have maps of Sodor and character sofas. Thomas themed meals are available and there is a great view of Mt Fuji which is literally right outside.

Outdoor pool
Free Wi-Fi
Non-smoking rooms
Restaurant on site
No elevator

Disney Resort Hotel character rooms

Located in Maihama the Disney Resort hotel has enchanting character themed rooms including the Alice in Wonderland room filled with playing cards, red roses and the Cheshire Cat, the Cinderella room fit for a princess, Beast's castle in the Beauty and the Beast room and the Tinkerbell room filled with leaves and trinkets. Tokyo Disneyland and Tokyo Bay are only a 5-minute walk away and hotel guests receive a 15-minute early entry into the theme park.

Free Wi-Fi
Outdoor pool
Restaurants on site
Non-smoking rooms
Bathtub in room
Coin operated laundry available onsite.

Art Hotel

Park Hotel's artwork rooms

Located in Shiodome, the Park hotel has 31 rooms on its artists floor decorated with intricate paintings that cover the walls, ceilings and even the furniture. You can sleep in a painting of an Onsen, a field of cherry blossoms, or under the shadow of Mount Fuji. Guests also have access to their own personal art concierge who will explain the meaning of each artwork.
If you are interested in art, the hotel also houses exhibits on several floors for guests to view.
Non-smoking and triple rooms are available, and the Ginza Art Gallery is located close by.

Free Wi-Fi
Two restaurants on site
Art shop on site
Coin operated laundry available.
Spa onsite

Chapter Five

Travelling with babies and children.

Travelling with babies

TIP Pack as lightly as you can. Japan is a very busy place, and your trip is likely to include a lot of walking and the use of public transport. Packing lightly will make transit more manageable, especially with babies and children.

What to pack

You may want to bring your own baby food, formula, wipes, and nappies/diapers. These are available in shopping centres, pharmacies, and convenience stores; however, they probably won't have the brands you are used to and the ingredients for the baby food will be written in Japanese.

Should I bring a pram or stroller?

This is a personal choice, though I recommend bringing a pram or stroller that will fold easily and is light to carry. There are many stairs in train and subway stations and not many have elevators. You'll be needing to carry the stroller up and down the stairs. Another aspect to be aware of is Japanese side streets do not usually have sidewalks or footpaths. Many attractions such as temples and shrines do not have ramps for your stroller.
Strollers can be hired by the hour from major department stores and some museums and art galleries if you do not want the trouble of bringing your own.

Breastfeeding in public

Breastfeed in generally not done in public in Japan, though you may be able to find a quiet place and use a shawl to cover. Many department stores have special nursing rooms and baby changing facilities where you can breastfeed in private if you prefer. Many also supply hot water to make baby formula.

Sleeping

Japanese hotel rooms are generally very small compared to Western rooms; however, most hotels will provide a cot for an extra fee providing there is enough room for one. Some hotels have triple rooms, but they are rare.

Baby changing areas

Department stores and larger train stations have baby changing rooms available for customers. Icons on the store floor map will show which floor they are located on or ask the customer service counter usually located on the first floor for assistance.

Many Japanese restrooms have a baby seat inside one of the cubicles to sit your baby in while you use the toilet. Much easier than having to balance your child on your lap!

Travelling with children.

Travelling with younger children can be a challenge as they often get tired and cranky and don't like waiting around boring places like airports and hotel lobbies. Let's face it, who does! The key is to make sure they are not overtired and have something to do.

Flying

Try to book flights that co-inside with your child's sleep time. For example, an afternoon flight where they can have an afternoon nap. That way, time will pass much faster and easier if your child can nap some of the way, and you might even get the chance to watch a movie or read a book!

If you are travelling on a long flight, an overnight option might be a good idea. This means they, (and you) can sleep for a few hours, making the flight go more quickly.

Take a change of clothes for each child in your carry-on luggage, in case of accidents. Also, bring a large plastic or zip-locked bag to place soiled clothes in if needed.

Pack some wet wipes for accidents and to freshen up.
I used to take a few favourite snacks from home on the flight with me, such as small crackers, mini packs of sultanas and small packets of tiny teddy biscuits.

Bring whatever your children usually like to snack on that is easily transportable. Although many airlines now have children's meals available, they may not always be available when your child is hungry, or they may be something your child doesn't like. A hungry toddler is not much fun.

Depending on the age of your baby or toddler, I used to take a couple of new items to entertain them. For example, a new baby book or toy, and for toddlers a lift the flap book style picture book and small new toy to engage them on the flight. Don't bring anything too noisy or disruptive, or with little pieces that may get lost between the seats!

Trains

There are over 1000 train lines in Tokyo, so you will probably be travelling on a train at some time during your holiday. We travelled by train almost daily and found them to be a quick and easy way to get around.

Keep in mind that long train trips can be very tiring for children. To make the journey a happier one, children might enjoy playing magnetic travel board games such as snakes and ladders, tick tack toe, draughts and even chess. These games are light weight and fold up to a small size which can fit in your hand luggage. Another idea is a pack of cards, they're small, lightweight and you can play numerous games with them. Children can also play with them while they're waiting at the airport or transit lounge.

Audiobooks are a good idea for a long train trip. Children can listen to their story whilst still being able to look outside the train windows and see some of the countryside.

Taxi

Taxis generally do not have baby/ child seats or carriers so you may wish to bear this in mind if travelling by taxi with young children and babies.

Toilets

Japan has some very cool toilets with numerous buttons for flushing, drying, music washing etc. Even for an adult knowing which button to press can be daunting, so I recommend helping your child when going to the toilet, so they don't press the wrong button and get a shock from an unexpected spray of water!

Not all Japanese toilets are ultra-modern, and some places use a squat toilet (hole in the ground type). You may need to help your child negotiate these.

Hygiene Face Masks

Although many people worldwide have become used to wearing facemasks for sickness, many Japanese people also wear face masks when they have allergies. Many people suffer from allergies to Cedar tree pollen (hay fever) especially in spring, and the masks help them to lessen the effects of the Cedar pollen.

Chapter Six

Top places to visit.

Tokyo has some amazing places to visit, all of them a little different. The city is divided into neighbourhoods or areas, and each area has its own distinct style. For example, Akihabara is very technology orientated and houses many of the gaming and electronic stores in Tokyo, Ginza is more upmarket with designer stores and Shibuya is the shopping centre with lots of trendy stores and neon lights.

Central Tokyo

Science Museum Takebashi

If you like science, you will enjoy visiting the Science Museum located in Kitanomaru Park, adjacent to the Imperial Palace in the heart of Tokyo. Interestingly, the museum stands on the remains of the northern area of Edo Castle and contains relics of the castle. There are five floors where you will find hands-on exhibits dealing with electricity, optical illusions, mechanics and more.

For drinks, snacks and science-related merchandise, there is a shop located on the 1st floor next to the ticket counter. Opening hours are 9.30 am-5 pm.

TIPS

Head to the fifth floor where you can watch the ultra-slow motion Jumping Grand Prix exhibit.

Entry is cash only.

Lockers are available on the 2nd and 4th floors.

https://www.jsf.or.jp/en/

Address: Chiyoda-Ku, Kitanomaru-Koen 2-1. Tokyo.

Hours: 9:30-16:50 (last entry 16:00). Closed some Wednesdays.

Closest Station: Takebashi Station.

Admission: General 880-yen; Junior/Senior High students 500-yen; elementary school 400-yen. Children under three are free. Cash only.

Tokyo Dome City

This interesting area has a lot of restaurants and cafes including many with western styles of food if you are craving a taste from home, including Sizzlers, Italian, Pizza, and Ice-cream! There is also a shopping area and amusement rides.

Dome Theater

Baseball

Baseball is an extremely popular spectator sport with the season beginning around the end of March and ending at the end of September. Most games are played in the evening and can be very entertaining and noisy with the crowd cheering loudly and animatedly. Tickets for a game can be purchased at the Dome, gate 22, convenience stores or through travel agents such as JBT.

Tokyo Dome City entertainment complex houses Japan's biggest indoor baseball stadium, the Tokyo Dome which seats over 40,000 people and is the home ground for professional baseball team the Yomiuri Giants. The Tokyo Dome is also used for a variety of other sporting and cultural events, including football, basketball, pro wrestling and music concerts. International performing artists often play at the Tokyo Dome. The baseball hall of fame and museum is also located here.

Also located at Tokyo City Dome is City Attractions is a recreation complex with numerous attractions including:

The Big O Ferris wheel where you can sing Karaoke while you ride 80 metres above the ground! There are 8 gondolas with the karaoke facility and songs are available in English, Korean, Chinese, and Japanese. The 15-minute ride costs 850-yen if not using a day pass. Children under 7 require an adult with them. A Skip Pass can be used on this ride.

Thunder Dolphin Rollercoaster. Not for the faint-hearted or those afraid of heights! This 1067-metre-long roller coaster starts with an 80-meter drop and has speeds of up to 130 km/h. Admission is 1,030-yen if not using a day pass. A Skip Pass can be used on this ride.

Haunted House ONRYOU ZASHIKI This haunted house is set in a classic Japanese-style house where the vengeful spirits of a couple who live there come after you from underneath the floor! Shoes must be removed before you step inside. Not for younger children or some adults #me! Ticket price: 850-yen / ride if day-pass not being used. A Skip Pass can be used on this ride.

Indoor bowling Centre for adults and older teenagers located in the CuBar lounge in the yellow building. Open 4-10.30 pm on weekdays, and 10 am-10.30 pm on Saturdays. Game fee for one game: Adults and students 850 yen, Junior high 15-years, or younger 700-yen. Rental shoe fee (size 15 cm to 32 cm available) is 400-yen and socks must be worn.
For further information, see the website.
www.tokyo-dome.co.jp/en/tourists/attractions/information

Space Museum TeNQ ("ten-cue") is an "entertainment museum" located on the 6th floor of the yellow building. The museum is full of audio-visual experiences looking at the mysteries of the universe and space travel, including a round 4K theatre. Exhibits are in Japanese and English.
https://www.tokyo-dome.co.jp/en/tourists/tenq/
Hours: 11 am-9 pm weekdays, 10 am-9 pm weekends.

1,800-yen for adults, 1,500-yen for high school and university students, 1,200-yen for 4 years old to junior high school. No admission to children under 4 years old.

Meets Port. This distinctive cylindrical building in Tokyo Dome City has five floors of restaurants, pubs, cafes, a Lawsons and 7-Eleven convenience stores. On the 3rd floor is a garden with a seating area.

TIPS

Generally, the restaurants and cafes open from 11 am until 11 pm. Most accept credit cards, some of the smaller establishments do not.

There are also cafes/restaurants located in the main hotel area, yellow building, attractions area and space (TeNQ) areas.

If you're wanting a coffee fix there is a Starbucks café, and if you are craving some western-style food the Baseball Café is a baseball themed restaurant serving western style dishes. Other western-style restaurants include TGI Fridays, Taco Bell, Denny's, and Sizzlers. There are also many ramen restaurants such as Kamukura, and dessert places serving crepes, cakes, and ice-cream. Plus, a food hall in the Go-Fun area.

For a list of the restaurants/ cafes and their locations, see.
www.tokyo-dome.co.jp/en/tourists/restaurants/

Shopping

As well as the museum, sports/entertainment complex, rides and games there are also shops available!
https://www.tokyo-dome.co.jp/en/tourists/dome/

Address: 1-3-61 Koraku, Bunkyo-Ku, Tokyo.
Hours: 10:00-21:00.
Closest Station: Korakuen, Suidobashi, Kasuga.
Admission: Free to enter Tokyo Dome City Attractions, however, a ticket is required for the rides either per attraction or with a one-day pass. A one-day pass costs 3,900-yen for adults, 3,400-yen for ages 12 to 17, 2,100-yen for ages 6 to 11.

TIPS

If you have shopping you don't want to carry around with you while you explore the area, you can leave your bags in a coin locker. There are several coin locker locations inside the Tokyo Dome area, including beside Gate 25 of Tokyo Dome and on the 1st floor of the Korakuen Hall Building, in La Qua.
Visit during the week for fewer crowds.
A Skip Pass can be purchased to skip the line for certain rides in the City Attractions area.
The Suidobashi Subway Station Exit 2 is right out front of the Meets Port (restaurant and café) building.

Koishigawa Korakuen Gardens

Depending on what time of the year you visit, this lovely green Japanese garden is filled with seasonal flowers and blossoms. For example, plum, camelia and cherry bloom in late spring, Lotus, hydrangea, and Iris flower in summer. We went in autumn and the trees were bright orange and red. There are bridges, walkways, and a pond with a walkway around it.

TIP There is also a garden tour available in English every Saturday at 10am and 1pm

https://www.stroll-tips.com/en/koishikawa-korakuen-gardens/

Address: 1-6-6 Koraku Bunkyo-Ku. Tokyo.

Hours: 9 am -5 pm (last entry 4.30 pm).

Admission: 300-yen, children under six free.

Beautiful autumn foliage

Ginza Graphics Gallery

If you love graphic design, you will enjoy the Ginza Graphics Gallery. The exhibits they display change regularly, and there is information on their website as to which project will be on show.

http://www.dnp.co.jp/gallery/ggg_e/
Address: DNP Ginza Building 7-7-2 Ginza, Chuo City, Tokyo.
Nearest Station: Tokyo Metro, Ginza Station, Exit A2, Tokyo Metro, Shimbashi Station, Exit 1, JR Shimbashi Station, Ginza line Exit A2.
Opening Hours: open 11 am -7 pm Mon to Sat closed Sundays.
Admission: Free.

Shiseido Gallery

Right next door to the Ginza Graphics Gallery is the Contemporary Shiseido Art Gallery housed in a tall red building. Located in the basement of the building, the gallery opened in 1919 and is the oldest in Japan. Information about the art is written in Japanese; however, the staff speak Japanese, Chinese and English if you have any questions.

https://www.shiseidogroup.com/gallery/access/access.html

Address: Basement floor (B1F) Tokyo Ginza Shiseido Building 8-8-3 Ginza, Chuo City, Tokyo. (Look for the tall, red building).
Nearest Station: Tokyo Metro Ginza Station Exit A2, Tokyo Metro Shimbashi Station Exit 1, JR Shimbashi Station Ginza line Exit A2.
Opening Hours: open 11 am -7 pm Tue to Sat. 10 am-7 pm Sundays. Closed Mondays.
Admission: Free.

Edo Tokyo Museum

The Edo-Tokyo Museum is a museum of Tokyo urban history, which exhibits the history, life, and culture of the city from the 1600's to today. The main exhibition is on the 5th and 6th floors and includes dioramas, costumes, life sizes figures and a replica of the Nihonbashi bridge and houses of the Edo period. I really enjoyed looking at all the figures in the dioramas and the display of fashion in Japan in the past.

There is a museum shop on site plus and Café and sit-down restaurant on the 1st floor. Opening hours are 10 am-6 pm.

Diorama in the Edo Museum

TIPS

There are free tours available in English. See the reception counter on the 6th floor to book one.

English audio guides are also available for a small refundable deposit.

Some of the special exhibition areas do not allow photography.

There are lounges available to use for free if you want to bring your own food.
Coin lockers are available on the 1st floor.

https://www.edo-tokyo-museum.or.jp/en/p-exhibition/

Address: 1-4-1 Yokoami, Sumida, Tokyo.
Hours: 9.30-5.30 pm Tue–Fri. 9.30-7.30 pm on Sat. Closed on Mondays.
Closest Station: 3-minute walk from West Exit of Ryogoku Station, JR Sobu Line.
Admission: Adults and children 12 years and over, 600-yen. Children younger than 12-years old, 300-yen.

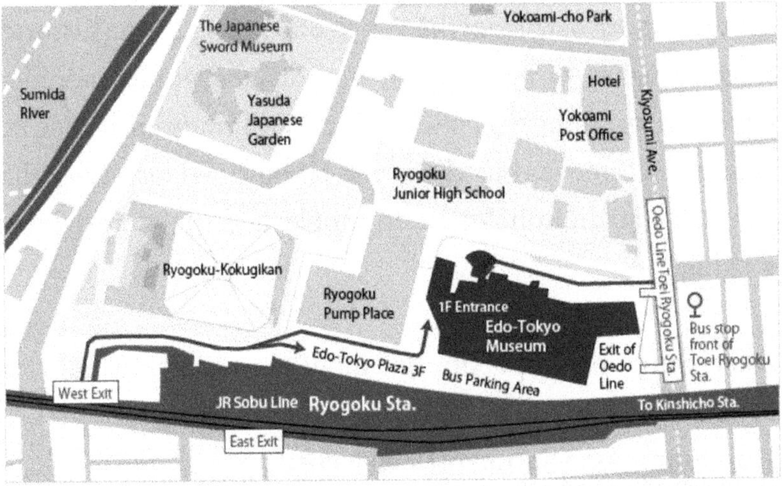
Yokoami-cho Park
The Japanese
Sword Museum
Sumida
River
Yasuda
Japanese
Garden
Hotel
Yokoami
Post Office
Kiyosumi Ave.
Ryogoku
Junior High School
Oedo Line Toei Ryogoku Sta.
Ryogoku-Kokugikan
Ryogoku
Pump Place
1F Entrance
Edo-Tokyo
Museum
Bus stop
front of
Toei Ryogoku
Sta.
Edo-Tokyo Plaza 3F
Bus Parking Area
Exit of
Oedo
Line
West Exit
JR Sobu Line
Ryogoku Sta.
To Kinshicho Sta.
East Exit

Sumo Wrestling at Ryogoku Kokogikan

Located a short walk from the Tokyo Edo Museum, the historical Ryogoku Kokogikan stadium is one of Japan's most eminent venues for watching Sumo wrestling. With traditional style box seating you remove your shoes and sit on cushions rather than chairs. The stadium holds 11000 people, and the atmosphere is amazing.

Tickets can be bought online one month in advance.

Japan Sumo Association official website

Address: 1-3-28 Yokoami, Sumida, Tokyo.
Closest Station: 3-minute walk from West Exit of Ryogoku Station, JR Sobu Line.

Akihabara

Anime, Manga, Gaming and Cosplay

There are many shops in Akihabara selling anime, manga, cosplay, and gaming products including Mandarake, K-Books and Sega.

For more information on shopping in Akihabara, see the Top Shopping Spot section.

No trip to Tokyo is complete without a visit to Akihabara or "Electric Town". Here you will find numerous electronics stores selling all kinds of electrical gadgets and devices. Akihabara is also home to all thing's *anime, manga, and gaming*. So, if you are into gaming, pop culture or anything *Otaku* (Japanese cartoon fantasy culture) this is the place to go.

Akihabara is also an amazing place to visit during the evening as all the neon shops and billboard signs will be lit up, making the area look like a scene from a sci-fi movie. Get your phone out for some cool photos!

Billboards in Akihabara

Be aware, when shopping for manga (comic books), if any manga is sealed in plastic, it usually means it contains adult content.

There are quite a few character themed cafes located in Akihabara, and they make a nice break from shopping.

Their drinks and food can be expensive for what you get; however, you are paying for the experience and surroundings. Some of the cafes require booking in advance.
See the section on Theme Cafes for more information.

Final Fantasy Café Eorzea

For fans of the Final Fantasy series, this café is located in Akihabara. Food and drinks are all related to the Final Fantasy series, and collectable coasters are given out when ordering.
See the Theme Cafes section for more information on the Final Fantasy café.

Address: Pasela Resort Akihabara. 1-1-10 Soto Kanda, 2nd Floor, Chiyoda-Ku, Tokyo.
Hours: you are allotted time slots of 2 hours (these are given out on a lottery-based system). 11.30- 10 pm.

Gashapon Kaikan

Gashapon are a type of vending machine similar to a gumball/bubblegum machine. They contain anime and video game characters or novelty toys in a tiny plastic bubble. And are usually 150-200 yen depending on the size, popularity, and rarity of the item inside. The collectable can be a badge, keyring, mini figure, or similar item. Gashapon machines can be found in front of bookstores, train stations, anime-related stores, and popular shopping spots.

Gashapon Kaikan is a store specializing in Gashapon and holds over 500 Gashapon machines. They have a large variety which changes monthly and includes rare Gashapon collectables. The store also sells figurines.

TIPS This store has a change machine to change yen notes into coins which is very useful if you don't have the correct coins needed. Ask the staff for help if you are having difficulty operating the machine as it is in Japanese.

Address: 3-15-5 Sotokanda, Chiyoda, Akihabara, Tokyo.
Closest Station: A seven-minute walk from JR Akihabara Station, Electric town Exit. Or a 2-minute walk from Tokyo Metro Suehirocho Station.
Admission: Free.

Rows of Gashapon machines

Colourful billboards in Akihabara

Godzilla Statue

If you are a fan of Godzilla, you can have a photograph with this statue (although small) of Godzilla. The Imperial Palace, Hibiya Park and Tokyo Kotsu Kaikan Shopping Complex are all located nearby.

Address: 3 Yurakucho, Chiyoda. Tokyo.
Hours: 24 hours.
Closest Station: JR Yurakucho Station, Yamanote Line Exit D8.
Admission: Free

Hibiya Park

Hibiya Park is a lovely place to have a break from shopping and sightseeing. There are colourful flower beds and tall trees such as Ginko and Japanese Apricot with blossoms during the spring and orange and red leaves during autumn. A great place for photographs. Around the park are several fountains, statues, and ponds, plus a children's playground. There are also drinking fountains to fill up your water bottle and an Information Centre.

www.tokyo-park.or.jp/park/format/map037.html

Address: 1-6 Hibiiya-koen, Hibiyakoen Tokyo.
Hours: Open 24 hours.
Closest Station: JR Yurakucho Station, Yamanote Line Exit D8. Hibiya Station.
Admission: Free.

Imperial Palace

As the Imperial Place is still in use by the Royal Family of Japan, it is not wholly open to the public. There are, however, some areas available to visit with a free tour. The tours are conducted in the morning and afternoons and last for approximately 75 minutes. See the website for details of times.

www.sankan.kunaicho.go.jp/multilingual/lang/en/information.html

TIPS

Tours are closed on Sundays and Mondays and certain times of the year. See the website for details. You will need to bring a valid form of identification such as a driver's license or passport (not photocopied) to the tour.

You can register for the walking tour in advance to ensure a spot or turn up on the day to see if any spots are available. Registration can be made on their website.

http://sankan.kunaicho.go.jp/multilingual/lang/en/koukyo/index.html

To join the tour on the day, you will need to bring your passport or driver's license to the Kikyo-mon gate of the Imperial Palace. You will then be asked to fill in a form. Numbered tickets will be distributed one hour prior to the starting time of the tour.

Imperial Palace East Garden

One of the most well-known gardens in Tokyo is the Imperial Palace East Garden (Kōkyo Higashi Gyoen), located in the heart of Tokyo. This public garden covers an area of about 210.000 square meters and has several different areas to enjoy.

Within the gardens is the remaining foundation of the former Edo Castle's main tower building. Once the tallest castle tower in Japan until a fire destroyed most of the main building in 1657.

There are also plumb trees which flower in spring, and an Iris flower garden.

Imperial Palace Garden

TIPS

There are maps in English, Japanese, Chinese, and Korean available.

There are three different entrance gates to the gardens, the Ōte-mon gate, the Hirakawa-mon gate and the Kitahanebashi-mon gate.

Address: 1-1 Chiyoda, Chiyoda, Tokyo.

Hours: 9 am- 4.30 pm. The hours differ depending on the season.

Closest Station: 10-minute walk from subway Chiyoda Line Nijubashi-mae Station, Exit 6. Mita Line, Otemachi Station, Exit D2.

15-minute walk from Tokyo Station, Marunouchi Central Exit.

Admission: Free.

Southern Tokyo

The southern part of Tokyo has many attractions to visit including the huge theme parks Disneyland and Disney Sea, plus the entertainment area Odaiba and Tokyo Tower.

Tokyo Bay

Disneyland

This was one of the first places we visited on our first trip to Tokyo. There was a lot to see and do, and the park can get very busy, so I recommend going early.
For more information on tickets and making restaurant bookings, as well as how to get to the park, any ride closures, and a downloadable map, see their website.

https://www.tokyodisneyresort.jp/en/tdl

Opening hours: 8 am or 9 am depending on the day until 10 pm.
Nearest Train Station: Maihama Station on JR (Japan Railway) Keiyo Line, Musashino Line.
Admission: One Day Pass Adult 7,500-yen, Junior 6,500-yen, Child 4,900-yen

Other passes are available, see website for details. Tickets can be purchased online.

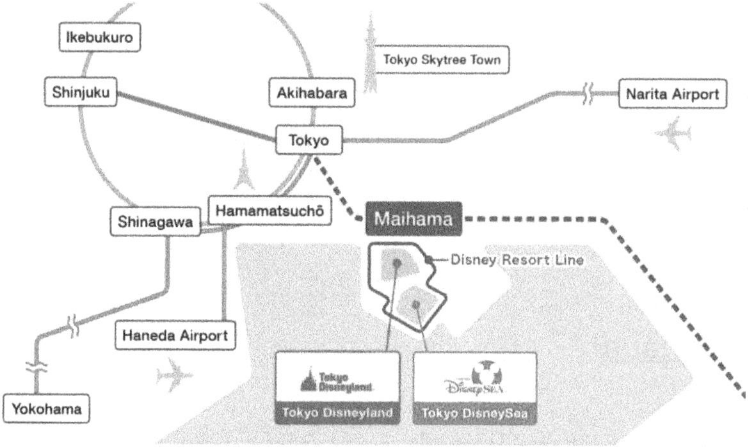

Location map of Disneyland and Disney Sea

TIPS

Plan your visit before you go. Look at the Disney Tokyo website and decide which rides and attractions you would most like to see. Some shows require pre-booking.
https://www.tokyodisneyresort.jp/en/tdl/

If you have a Fast Pass the queues on some rides can be shortened. We used a Fast Pass, and it was fantastic and well worth getting.

If you know which day you would like to go, book your ticket online in advance.

Grab a map of the park which shows the rides, attractions, shops and restaurants. Maps can be downloaded from the Disneyland website or found in the park where Wagons containing maps are located at the left and right of World Bazaar.

Have a designated place to meet just in case anyone gets lost!

Try not to visit on the weekend or on a public holiday as it will be very crowded.

Coin-operated lockers 400-800 yen depending on the size are available around the park entrance area.

Don't lose your park entrance ticket! You will need these to ride on any of the Fast Pass rides.

You can book restaurants ahead of time online on the Disney website if you know where you want to eat in advance.

How to use a Fast Pass in the park.

Obtain a Fast Pass for each person in your party when you enter the park. Located in a booth on the right side as you enter the park.

Go to the Fast Pass ride you wish to ride on first (only some rides in the park are Fast Pass ride. See the section below on individual rides to find out which rides offer the Fast Pass system). Check the next available time to ride on the Fast Pass board next to the ride entrance.
Go to the Fast Pass distribution area and scan your park admission ticket onto the reader of the Fast Pass machine. You will be given a Fast Pass reminder ticket of when you need to return to go on your ride. Note, each person needs to scan their own park entrance ticket.

Return to the ride at your designated time. If you miss the time printed on your Fast Pass reminder, your Fast Pass will be invalid, and you will have to choose another time.

Skip the "long" standard entry queue and go to the Fast Pass entrance. Scan your entrance park ticket (not the Fast Pass reminder ticket) and get ready to ride!

Statue of Walt Disney

Park Themed Areas

There are seven different themed areas in Disney Land Tokyo, each with restaurants, shops, rides, and attractions to match. The seven themed areas are:

World Bazaar

Adventureland

Westernland

Critter Country

Fantasyland
Toontown
Tomorrowland

The areas also have different food booths and wagons serving ice-cream, drinks, hotdogs, popcorn, and other snacks, as well as shops selling merchandise related to the theme or Disney in general. These include hats and headbands, candies, Stationery, plushies and other toys and souvenirs.

TIP

If you enjoy popcorn, there are popcorn vendors selling many varieties of popcorn, including soy sauce, caramel, curry, strawberry, honey, chocolate, and other flavours of popcorn throughout the park. It's a popcorn lovers paradise!

Disney Sea

We went to Disney Sea as a family and had a great time. We managed to go on our four favourite rides with minimal waiting time using the Fast Pass system and enjoyed walking around and looking at all the different areas the rest of the time.

For more information on tickets and making restaurant bookings, as well as how to get to the park, any ride closures, and a downloadable map, see their website.
https://www.tokyodisneyresort.jp/en/tdl.

Opening hours: 8 am or 9 am depending on the day until 10 pm.
Nearest Train Station: Get off at Maihama Station on JR (Japan Railway) Keiyo Line, Musashino Line.
Admission: One Day Pass Adult 7,500-yen, Junior 6,500-yen, Child 4,900-yen
Other passes are available, see website for details. Can be bought online.

Note that the attractions and rides are in Japanese.

Disney sea at night

TIPS for making the most of your day:

Look at the website and decide in advance which rides you most want to go on the most (aim for 3 or 4 rides).

Don't visit on a weekend as it will be very crowded.

Go early. Aim to get there as soon as the park opens for your best shot at getting onto rides.

Most importantly make use of the Fast Pass system, it's a great time saver. As soon as we arrived in the park, we headed straight to the Indiana Jones ride which was on top of our *to do ride list* and got a fast pass (you need one for each person going on the ride, just use your park entrance ticket in the Fast Pass machine).

Your ticket will show which time you need to come back to go on your ride. While we were waiting for our allocated time slot for that particular ride, we managed to get on another less popular ride.

Buy your tickets online before you go so you don't have to queue for tickets to get in.

Grab a map of the park. It will show you where the rides, shops, restaurants, and attractions are. Maps can be downloaded from the Disney Sea website and found in the park. Wagons containing maps are located on either side of Passaggio MiraCosta.

Coin-operated lockers 400-800 yen depending on the size are available around the park entrance area.

You can book restaurants ahead of time online on the Disney website if you know where you want to eat in advance.

As long as you plan ahead and get there early, you can get onto quite a few rides. It was great fun to see everyone dressed up wearing different hats and Mickey ears, and if you like popcorn they have about 6 different types, including cappuccino!

How to use a Fast Pass in the park.

Obtain a Fast Pass for each person in your party when you enter the park. Located in a booth on the right side as you enter the park.

Go to the Fast Pass ride you wish to ride on first (only some rides in the park are Fast Pass ride. See the section below on individual rides to find out which rides offer the Fast Pass system). Check the next available time to ride on the Fast Pass board next to the ride entrance.

Go to the Fast Pass distribution area and scan your park admission ticket onto the reader of the Fast Pass machine. You will be given a Fast Pass reminder ticket of when you need to return to go on your ride. Note, each person needs to scan their own park entrance ticket.

Return to the ride at your designated time. If you miss the time printed on your Fast Pass reminder, your Fast Pass will be invalid, and you will have to choose another time.

Skip the "long" standard entry queue and go to the Fast Pass entrance. Scan your entrance park ticket (not the Fast Pass reminder ticket) and get ready to ride!

FastPass for a ride at Disney Sea

Park Themed Areas

Like Disneyland, Tokyo Sea has seven themed areas, each with its own rides, attractions, and restaurants to match the theme. Reservations for some restaurants can be made online https://www.tokyodisneyresort.jp/en/tdl

The seven themed areas in Disney Sea are:
Mediterranean Coast
Arabian Coast

Mermaid Lagoon
Mysterious Island
Lost River Delta
Port Discovery
American Waterfront

Indiana Jones Raging Spirits ride.

Tokyo Tower

This Tower built just after WW2 used to be the highest in Tokyo (now taken over by the Sky Tree). If the weather is fine, you can get a 360-degree view of Tokyo, including Mt Fuji. At night the tower is lit up with over 180 lights. In Summer (July -September) there is a cool white version of the lights and in winter, (October -July) there is a warm orange version.

In 2019 an extra light display was set up to light up the tower on Friday and Saturday nights using 268 LED lights with 12 different colours. This runs from 8 pm-12 pm and changes design every hour.

There are two observation decks, one at 150 m on the main deck and one at 250 m on the top deck.

Foot town is on the lower levels of the tower.

Level 1 Foot town has a ticket office, information counter and the One-Piece store and Café.

Level 2 has a Lawson's convenience store, food courts, cafes and restaurants including burgers, pizza, and ice-cream. There are also souvenirs available on this level.

Level 3 is the entrance and ticket counter for One Piece Tower (See more information on this below).

Level 4-5 houses One-Piece Tower.

TIPS

The Top-deck tour includes a welcome drink, history tour and audio guide, which is very useful if you want to know what you are looking at.

If you purchase your combo ticket for the main observation and top decks online, there is a discount of 20- yen per person.

If you go in the late afternoon you will get to see a view of Tokyo during the day and at the start of the evening as the lights of the city light up.

Coin lockers are available on the first floor of *Foot Town*.

Right next door to the tower is Shiba Park and Zojoji Buddhist Temple where you can see the Tokyo Tower in its full form. This is a good place to see the tower when it is lit up at night.

www.tokyotower.co.jp/en.html
Address: 1-6-1 Daiba, Minato-Ku, Tokyo.
Hours: 9 am-11 pm.
Closest Station: Akabanebashi Station, Oedo line.
Admission:
Main deck only Adults 1200-yen. Children 6-18 years old, 700-yen. Children 4-6 years old 500-yen.
Main deck and Top deck combination. Adults 3000-yen. Children 6-18 years 2000-yen. Children 4-6 years 1400-yen.

Tokyo Tower in the evening

Street Kart Tokyo Bay

Street Kart Tokyo Bay is a 1.5 to 3 hour driving tour where you get to explore different areas throughout Tokyo, including Shibuya Crossing, Tokyo Tower, and Rainbow Bridge by go-cart! A guide goes with you to show you the way and another helper takes photos of everyone as you drive throughout the city. Once you check-in, you change into costumes (onesies) which you can either borrow or bring your own. You are then shown how to operate the cars and off you go. This was a really fun activity and a great break from walking to see the sights. My teenagers loved it.

Reservations can be made online or through a tour company such as JR travel.

TIP

**A valid driver's license (from your home country) and passport are needed to use the Go-carts. Arrive 10 minutes before your allocated booking time as they start exactly on time. Lockers are provided for your belongings.

https://kart.st/tokyobay.html

Address: 2-10 Shinkiba Koutoh, Tokyo.

Email tokyobay@kart.st.

Hours: 10 am-10 pm.

Nearest Station: JR Tokyo Bay Station.

Admission:10'000-yen per person 1.5 to 2-hour session.

Odaiba

Odaiba is an artificial island in Tokyo Bay with a lot to do. There are several shopping complexes, theme cafes, innovative museums, and gaming centres. Many of the attractions are located close to each other, which makes it easy to visit a few in one day.

Yurikamome Line (Driverless Train)

The most interesting way to get to Odaiba is on the driverless Yurikamome Train. The train leaves from Shinbashi Station, and travels along an elevated track which curves above the waters of Tokyo Bay, crosses over the Rainbow Bridge and goes around Odaiba. The train is a fully automated, computer-operated train that travels at a moderate speed which gives you lots of opportunities to take photographs and to get an exciting view.
The cost of a one-way ticket from Shinbashi Station to Daiba Station, which is where most of the entertainment is costs 320-yen.

TIP

The best seat on the Yurikamome Train is in the front carriage, where you will get an uninterrupted, driver's eye view. Be on the platform early if you plan on sitting in the front carriage, however, as it's a popular seat.

Yurikamome Driverless Train

Walk Across Rainbow Bridge

The Rainbow Bridge stretches across from Tokyo Bay to Odaiba. During the day the bridge is white, and at night it is illuminated with a kaleidoscope of colours. Pedestrians are able to walk across the bridge on the Rainbow Promenade from either side. The northern walkway has views of the Tokyo Sky Tree and Tokyo Tower, and the southern walkway has panoramas of Tokyo Bay.

TIP

To walk across the bridge, go to the Rainbow Bridge Entrance and catch the elevator to the seventh floor. The walk takes half an hour to an hour, and you will hear some traffic noise.

Address: Shibaura Anchorage. 3-33-19 Kaigan, Minato City. Tokyo.
Hours: April to October 9:00 am – 9:00 pm, November to March 10:00 am – 6:00 pm. Closed on the 3rd Monday of the month.
Closest Station: Shibaura-futō.
Admission: Free.

View across Rainbow Bridge

LegoLand

If you like Lego, you will love visiting LegoLand in Tokyo. The activity centre is located in the Decks Tokyo Beach Island Mall in Odaiba and consists of a Lego mini-land showcasing Lego designs and Lego building and creative areas where your children can use Lego to build and create. There is also a 4D cinema, Lego rides and games, a shop and café with food and drink.

https://tokyo.legolanddiscoverycenter.jp/en/

Address: 1-6-1 Daiba, Minato Tokyo.
Hours: 10:00-21:00 (last entry 19:00).
Closest Station: Odaiba Kaihin Koen, Tokyo Teleport.
Admission: 2,200-yen per person.

TIP

The Trick Art Museum is located nearby so you can visit both in one day.

Tokyo Trick Art Museum

The Tokyo Trick Art Museum is tucked away in the Seaside Mall in Odaiba. If you are visiting the area, then it is worth taking an hour to go to find this little place tucked into a busy mall (Daiba I-Chome Shotengai) that is filled with a lolly shop, trinkets, and video games.

You buy a ticket at the vending machine to the right of the entrance and queue up. A guide will give you instructions. Then you are left on your own to explore. The price was 1000 yen when we visited and takes about an hour to go through. Once inside, there are many painted illustrations and instructions next to each picture so visitors can position themselves in the right place to be part of the illusion. This is good fun for all ages.

http://www.trickart.info/english/index.html

Address: 1-6-1 Daiba, Minato- Tokyo.
Hours: 11:00-21:00
Closest Station: Odaiba Kaihin Koen, Daiba
Admission: 1000-yen adults, 700-yen children.

San Rio World

If you are a fan of Hello Kitty and her friends, you'll enjoy visiting the two-story San Rio store in Ginza. Cuteness abounds in this store full of plushies and other collectables.

Address: 1at and second floors Nishi Ginza Department store 4-1 Saki, Ginza, Chuo-Ku
Hours: 11-8pm
Closest Station: Ginza Station

Joypolis

Joypolis is an indoor amusement centre located in the Decks Tokyo Beach Island Mall in Odaiba. This Sega-orientated theme park is one of the biggest indoor amusement parks in Japan and is packed with games, virtual reality rides and 3D attractions for ages seven and older. You can simulate riding a snowboard, riding a hang glider, or going on a virtual roller coaster. There is also a real whirling rollercoaster called the Spin Bullet which rotates 360 degrees!
There are virtual reality games where you battle enemies or get spooked in the Mystic Mansion or Room of the Living Doll. The names say it all! (These ones are better for older children).

Entrance to Joypolis Amusement Centre

TIPS

Joypolis like many attractions in Tokyo, gets super busy, so I suggest buying your entrance ticket online in advance from their website.

Also, note that it is better to wear contact lenses rather than glasses for the 3D rides.

If you have long hair, make sure you tie it back and be prepared to line up for the rides!

Go on a weekday afternoon for fewer people.

Only buy a day pass if you think you will be at the park for a half-day or more. If you only want to go on a few rides, it's better value for money to pay the entrance admission, then pay for each individual ride.
If you are coming in the evening (after 5 pm), the Night Passport is exceptionally good value. It gives you access to the amusement park for five hours, from 5 pm to 10 pm and costs 1000 yen less than the standard admission price.

Joypolis, The Trick Art Museum and Madame Tussauds are located in the same area, so if you have the energy, all can be visited in one day.

*** if you bring your passport when purchasing tickets, you can get a 300-yen discount on entry ticket!

https://tokyo-joypolis.com/language/english/

Address: 1-6-1 Daiba, Minato, Tokyo.
Hours: 10:00-22:00. Last entry 9.15 pm.
Closest Station: Odaiba Kaihin Koen, Daiba.
Admission: Basic 800-yen adults, 300-yen children (7-17 years) rides are pay as you go. Or Day pass with unlimited rides 4300-yen adults and 3500-yen children (7-17 years). Night pass (after 5pm) 3500-yen adults, 2500-yen children.
Tickets may also be purchased online in combo with other attractions such as the Giant Ferris Wheel in Palette town or Madame Tussauds.

Shiba Park and Zojoji Temple

This is a peaceful park where you can get a great view of Tokyo Tower from a distance and see the whole structure.
The Zojoji Buddhist Temple is dedicated to Children. It is a very peaceful area with lots of shrines, statues, and a lovely teahouse.

Address: 4-7-35 Shibakoen Minato-Ku. Tokyo.
Hours: 9 am-5 pm.
Closest Station: Shibakoen Station, Mita Subway Line. Daimon Station, Oedo Subway Line. Ten-minute walk from Hamamatsucho Station, JR Yamanote line.
Admission: Free.

Fuji TV building light show.

Several times throughout the year the outside of the Fuji TV building is lit up with 700 LED lights in a fantastic display of lights and sound.

TIP

If you happen to be in Tokyo when one of the light shows is scheduled to run, make sure you're on ground level for nightfall and at the right distance from the building to appreciate the fantastic show. Not only does the building light up, but the whole show is synchronized to music from popular Fuji TV shows.

If you want to go inside the Fuji TV building, it is free and closes at 5.30 pm (closed on Monday). Entry to the giant sphere on the 25th floor costs extra.

https://www.fujitv.com/visit_fujitv/

Address: 2-4-8 Daiba, Minato City, Tokyo.
Hours: 10 am -5.30 pm. Closed on Mondays.
Closest Station: Daiba Station on the Yurikamome Line, or Tokyo Teleport on the Rinkai Line. 20-minute walk across Rainbow Bridge.
Admission: Free. Hachitama Spherical Observation room is extra. 700-yen Adults, Children over 6 years-old 450-yen.

Miraikan, National Museum of Emerging Science & Innovation

At the Miraikan, National Museum of Emerging Science & Innovation, you get the opportunity to have an interactive, hands-on experience with science.
There are three permanent exhibition areas, Explore the Frontiers, Create your own future, and Discover your Earth. There is also a Dome theatre which shows films relating to science several times a day.

The Explore the Frontiers exhibition allows you to explore space, our solar system and the Earth. For example, you can examine how exploring the universe on space missions affects life on earth.

In the Create your Future Zone, you can interact with Alter, an advanced android, or communicate with other people through her while you manipulate her reactions. There are also live performances from Asimo, the most advanced humanoid robot technology available. Asimo is being developed for the purpose of helping sufferers of disabilities with routine household tasks. There are shows four times a day at 11.00/13.00/14.00/16.00.

Asimo in action at the Miraikan, National Museum of Emerging Science & Innovation

The Discover our Earth zone has a suspended globe of the Earth made from tiny LED panels. There are interactive displays and models all relating to the Earth and how people affect our environment.

The museum shop is located on the first floor and is open from 10 am to 6 pm. Closed Tuesdays.

The Miraikan restaurant is a self-service facility located on the 7th floor and is open 10 am- 5pm, closed on Tuesdays. On the 5th floor is the Miraikan café which serves hot and cold drinks and snacks.

TIP

For an even more surreal experience, download the free Miraikan notebook smartphone app_before visiting the museum. The app includes an audio guide, allows you to take AR (augmented reality) photos and take a quiz.

https://www.miraikan.jst.go.jp/en/

Address: 2-3-6 Aomi, Koto-Ku, Tokyo.
Hours: 10 am -5 pm. Closed on Tuesdays.
Closest Station: 5-minute walk from Tokyo International Cruise Terminal Station or a 4-minute walk from Telecom Center Station.
Admission: adults 630-yen, under 18 years-old 230-yen. Dome theatre admission adults 310-yen, 18 years and younger 100-yen. Admission tickets can be purchased from the outside ticket booth or 3rd floor information counter.

Happoen Gardens Minato

We found this small, lovely garden full of maple, bonsai and cherry trees, bridges, lanterns, and statues. There are walkways and ponds with large orange and white Koi fish, and the park is a peaceful place to recharge from the hectic streets of Tokyo. One of the paths had a bonsai display which was interesting to see. There is also a 200-year-old tea house, and we saw several couples getting married (some areas may be roped off for wedding ceremonies). It's a good place to witness a traditional wedding ceremony if you go on the weekend.

Koi fish in Happoen Gardens Minato

https://happo-en.com/banquet/about/

Address: 1-1-1 Shirokanedai, Minato. Tokyo.

Hours: 10 am-10.30 pm.

Closest Station: Shirokanedai Station, Toei Mita Line.

Admission: Free.

Visit the Panasonic Centre

If you're looking for a break from spending money (and who isn't!) there's one place to go in Odaiba, the Panasonic Centre. A cross between an exhibition centre and interactive museum, there's enough to keep you occupied for hours, and it's nearly all free.
On the first floor is an *Active Learning Camp* showing everything related to the Olympic and Paralympic Games. There's also a showroom of Panasonic products from the past and ones which are still in development but coming in the future.

The second floor has the RiSuPia museum where you can learn some interesting facts about space. This floor also concentrates on Nintendo and past and present Nintendo games. Note to give everyone a chance to play; games times are limited to 20 minutes each game (less if there is a queue waiting to play). The E-Feel Café is also located on this floor serving drinks and snacks.

On the third floor is the RiSuPia Discovery Centre. This centre delves into what museums will look like in the future. Every visitor has their own handset to allow for interaction with the exhibits. There is also a Magical Performance Theatre showing 3D information-based programs.

TIP

There are coin lockers available if you want to store any shopping or belongings, making it easier to wander around the exhibits and game areas.

https://www.panasonic.com/global/corporate/center/tokyo/floor.html

Address: 3-5-1 Ariake, Koto-Ku, Tokyo.
Hours: 10 am-6.30 pm. Closed on Mondays.
Closest Station: Kokusai-Tenjijo Station on Rinkai Line. Ariake Station on Yurikamome.
Admission: Free. Entry to the RiSuPia exhibition on the third-floor costs 500-yen for adults, children free.

Team Lab Planets Digital Art Museum

The Teamlab Digital Art Museum is a fairly new fun museum in Tokyo and a great place to visit.
This is an amazing interactive experience that combines sensory perception and digital art. Over five hundred computers relay images via four hundred and seventy projectors to create these sensory effects with light and sound.

****The museum has multiple worlds to explore. (these will change depending on the year and season so check their website for further information)**

The worlds we saw included:

Drawing on the water. Walk through shallow water amongst colourful digital Koi fish. The fish change into seasonal flowers as you brush past them.

The infinite crystal luminance. Dots of colour are used to create a picture and 3 dimensional objects in this artwork. Use your smartphone to select elements in the universe.

Floating in the fairy universe of flowers. Sit or lie in the space as you are surrounded by digital falling flowers. Interactions between yourself and the artwork causes the art to change.

Dimensional existence. This space is filled with large spheres of free-floating light. The spheres change colour as you touch and brush past them.

Waterfall of light This artwork is based on the natural waterfall in the mountains of Shikoku. Light reflects off the particles of water that make up the waterfall. Walk barefoot towards the waterfall to see the cascading, shining particles.

Soft black hole. As you walk through this artwork your feet sink down into soft cushioned material. The space changes with the weight of people's bodies. (May not be suitable for younger children or people with ankle, knee, or hip injuries)

Floating flower garden. Sit or walk amongst the 3-dimensional mass of flowers surrounding you with flowers also reflected on the mirrors below you.

Moss Garden. This artwork is located outside. Silver orbs fill up the green moss garden and emit sounds when touched. If you see them after sunset, they look very cool as the orbs change colour and glow purple, green, pink and blue.

TIPS

Buy your admission tickets online well in advance. The museum has limited tickets available and is extremely popular. There are no door sales at this time.

The wait times to enter, even with a pre-purchased ticket, can be at least 30 mins. If you must leave the queuing line, leave one person from your group in place to hold your spot or ask an attendant for assistance.

An App is available to download which explains each piece of artwork.

https://www.planets.teamlab.art/tokyo/
Address: Toyosu 6-1-16, Koto-ku Tokyo.
Hours: 10-8pm last entrance 1 hour before closing time.
Closest Station: Shin-Toyosu station. Waterfront Yurikamome Line
Or Tokyo Metro station Yukaucho Line
Admission: 3200-yen for adults, 2000 yen for high school children, 1000-yen for children.

Exhibition at Team Labs

Yokohama

Cup a Noodle Museum

The cup a noodle museum is an interactive museum where you can learn about Mr Momofuku Ando, who was the creator of a *cup-a-noodles* and *chicken ramen* and make your own cup a noodle!

The museum was well organised, and during our visit, we created our own Cup-a-Noodle, enjoyed a video presentation of the history of Cup-a-Noodle with free English language headsets, had fun in the Noodle Park and enjoyed our lunch at the Noodle Bazaar.

In the Chicken Ramen section, you can learn to make Ramen noodles by hand. The lesson is for 90 minutes, and you get to take your noodles home with you. To do this, you need to reserve a place, and children must be 6 years old. The session times are: 10:15 / 11:00 / 11:45 / 13:15 / 14:00 / 14:45 / 15:30 / 16:15. Adults and children over 12 years 500-yen, children 300-yen.

In the Cup a Noodle Factory you can create your own cup a noodle. Using a cup, you colour, you then choose your own soup flavour, and add toppings. Altogether, there are 5,460 flavour combinations.

TIPS

go during the week (not on a Tuesday as they are closed!) to beat the crowds.

Free English, Chinese and Korean headsets are available if you require them (2000-yen bond).

There are coin lockers available on the first floor.

https://www.cupnoodles-museum.jp/en/yokohama/

Address: 2-3-4 Shinko, Naka, Yokohama.
Hours.10 am-6 pm Wed-Mon. Closed Tuesdays.
Closest Station: 12-minute walk from the JR/Shieichikatetsu Sakuragicho Station.
8-minute walk from the Minatomirai line Minatomirai Station.
Admission: Adults 500 yen, children free. Chicken Ramen factory, Adults, and children over 12 years 500 yen, children 300 yen. Cup a noodle factory 300-yen per "cup a noodle" made.

Northern Tokyo

Ikebukuro

Ikebukuro is a large area with two giant department stores, Sunshine City and Parco. There are a lot of places to shop and see in this area, including Otome Road (Maiden Road) which is an area dedicated to mainly female anime culture.

Sunshine Aquarium

This little aquarium is situated on top of the Sunshine City shopping complex. There are three floors, including an outdoor "Marine Garden" where you can view the penguins from above, the Sunshine Aqua Ring with its view of sea lions swimming overhead, and the dreamlike "Jellyfish Tunnel.

All of the exhibits and tanks were clean (some of the tanks could have been a little bigger) and the environment was peaceful and very family friendly. It's not too big, so it doesn't take the entire day to visit. Perfect for spending a few hours. The aquarium holds various events throughout the day such as penguin feeding, sealions shows and divers entering the tank. There are

free pamphlets in various languages available for visitors which we found helpful.
The fish and animals housed here include dolphins, octopus, eels, piranhas, sea horses, sea otters, seals, and giant crabs.
https://sunshinecity.jp/en/aquarium/

TIPS

Map of the Aquarium

https://sunshinecity.jp/en/aquarium/information/floor_map.html

There are a café and shop selling aquarium toys etc. available.

To help skip the queue, tickets can be pre-purchased at Family Mart, 7-Eleven and Circle K Convenience stores. (Elevators to reach the main entrance may still have a line).

Starbucks, Tully's coffee, and several Family Mart convenience stores are all located close by for snacks and drinks.

Address: Rooftop of World Import Mart Building, Sunshine City. 3-1 Higashi-Ikebukuro, Tokyo.,
Hours: 10 am-6 pm.
Closest Station: Ikebukuro Station, Exit 35. Walk down Sunshine 60 Street towards Sunshine City complex.

Yurakucho Line's Higashi-Ikebukuro Station Exits 6 and 7. This takes you through an underground passage to the Aquarium. Look for information on the route next to the Toys r Us store.
Admission: Adults 2200-yen, Children 6 and older, 1200-yen, children 4 and older, 700-yen, children under three, free.

Pokémon Centre

If you have a passion for Pokémon, then visiting this store is a must. The store is full of plushies, video games, collectables and everything Pokémon including Pokémon kitchen utensils! Even the cash registers are in the shape of Poke balls!

Address: 3-1-2 Higashiikebukuro 2nd floor Sunshine City. Ikebukuro. Tokyo.
Hours: 10 am-8 pm.
Closest Station: Ikebukuro Station, Exit 35. Walk down Sunshine 60 Street towards Sunshine City complex.

Round One Entertainment Complex

This is a 24-hour entertainment complex located in Ikebukuro. There is also one located in Osaka and Kyoto. The lower three floors have arcade games with retro-style games such as Space Invaders and Mario Kart. There is also a JR train simulator available. The upper floors house a bowling alley, Billiards (pool) table Karaoke and table tennis (ping pong).
Food and drinks are available to purchase.

TIPS

Take cash as when we went there weren't any credit card facilities available at the time.

You can bring your own headphones to plug into the games if you wish, and there is free WIFI available.

The instructions for the games are in Japanese; however, the staff are friendly and happy to help you if you ask them.

Address: 1-14-1 Ikebukuro Square, Higashi-Ikebukuro, Toshima-Ku, Tokyo.
Hours: Open 24 hours!
Closest Station: Toshima Station, East Exit.

Animate Ikebukuro

This is the main Animate store and has nine floors of Anime related items. There are also regular exhibits and events held here. Their website listed below has a calendar of events being held throughout the year. The website is in Japanese at this time so you will need to translate with Google translate or similar. www.animate.co.jp/

Address: 1-20-7 Higashi-Ikebukuro, Toshima-Ku, Tokyo.
Hours: 10 am - 9 pm.

Animate Ikebukuro

Otome Road

Otome Road or Maiden Road is a lot like Akihabara; however, it caters to female anime fans. The 200-meter-long street is filled with shops carrying merchandise targeted towards women. Otome Road is Ikebukuro's go-to place for anime-related merchandise such as cosplay costumes, manga, plushies, doujinshi merchandise and figurines. Animate, Mandarake, K-Books, and Lashinban all have stores in this area.
(For more information on Otome Road see the shopping section).
Address: 3 Higashi-Ikebukuro, Toshima-ku, Tokyo.

Tokyu-Hands

Tokyo Hands sells a little bit of everything. It's a great place to browse for inexpensive and interesting Japanese' products and items that you may not see in the shops at home.
This branch in Ikebukuro is a superstore with 8 floors worth of various goods from cute erasers to animal-shaped onigiri rice moulds.
If you like cats, there is a cat café called Nekobukuro on the 8th floor!
Address: 1-28-10 Higashi-Ikebukuro, Toshima-Ku, Tokyo.
Hours: 10 am-9 pm.
Nearest Station: Ikebukuro Station, East Exit.

Book and Bed

If you're looking for something quirky and fun in Ikebukuro, drop into Book and Bed. Book and Bed is a library, reader's nook, and place to sleep all rolled into one! Customers sleep or relax on the beds amongst the 5000 books. There are both Japanese and English books available to read.

There are two floors available, with bookshelves and reading/sleeping beds on each floor. You can choose between an overnight stay or just a day check-in to experience this book haven. Rates are charged by the hour during the day, so you can stay and enjoy the books for a short time if you wish.

TIPS

WIFI is free.

An electrical outlet (you will need an adapter for overseas appliances), slippers, earplugs, lockers, reading light and privacy curtain, are provided for overnight stays.

Payment by Credit card or IC cards (e.g. Pasmo) only, no cash.

Reservations are not accepted for day-time visitors, drops in only. Reservations are available for overnight stays.

The accommodation is simple, and 24-hour shared toilets and showers are available.

www.bookandbedtokyo.com/en/tokyo/

Address: Lumiere Building, 7th floor. 1-17-7 Nishi-Ikebukuro, Toshima-Ku, Tokyo.
Cost: 4600-yen per night. 500-yen per hour not including tax.
Hours: 1 pm-8 pm for daytime visits. Check the website for overnight stay times.

Bed and Book

Ueno

Tokyo Ueno zoo

Ueno Zoo is the oldest zoo in Japan and houses 3000 animals! Their animals include Giant Pandas, polar bears, nocturnal animals and a children's zoo with guinea pigs, rabbits, cows and goats. The Ueno Zoo has an active breeding program of endangered animals.
There is a gift shop at the zoo selling animal plushies, snacks and Stationery.

TIPS

Ameya Yokocho shopping street is nearby and handy for a lunch stop before or after the zoo or to purchase snacks to take with you into the zoo.

Go during the week, if possible, when the zoo will be less busy.

The zoo has free Wi-Fi "Free_wi-fi_and TOKYO".

You can bring your own food, or there are a snack bar and cafeteria with tables and chairs.
coin lockers are available.

https://www.tokyo-zoo.net/english/ueno/index.html

Address: Ueno Koen Taito, Tokyo.

Hours: 9:30-19:00 (closed on Mondays).

Closest Station: The main gate is 5 minutes' walk from Ueno Station, Park Exit.

Admission: Adults and children over 16 years of age 600-yen., Children 13-15 years of age 200-yen. Children 12 and under free.

Ueno Park

Ueno Park is a large public park with easy access from Ueno Station. The park has many spacious areas and is a great place to take a break from the hustle and bustle of Tokyo.
There are park benches to sit on and fountains to enjoy. Ueno Park has over 1000 cherry trees and is a prime spot for cherry blossom viewing in late March and early April. People hold cherry blossom viewing parties (Hanami) in the park during this time. There are also tulips in winter.

Besides the parkland, Ueno Park has many museums on its grounds including the Tokyo National Museum (see below) the National Science Museum and the Tokyo Metropolitan Art Museum. The Ueno Zoo is also located within Ueno Park as are several temples and shrines listed below:

Kaneiji Temple remnants are located in the northwest corner of the park. Open 9-5pm, free entry.
Kiomizu Kannon Temple was built in 1631, open 9-5 pm, free entry.
Toshogu Shrine was built in 1616, open 9-4.30 pm, 500-yen for entry to the inner shrine, otherwise, free.
Bentendo Temple is located on an island in Shinobazu Pond at the southern end of the park. The temple is dedicated to Benten, (not the tv show!) the goddess of good fortune, wealth, music, and knowledge. This is a very popular spot during the cherry

blossom season when the grounds are crowded with festival food stalls. Open 9-5 pm, free entry.

TIPS

There is a Starbucks located near the National Museum in Takenodai Square if you are in need of a coffee fix.

Row boats, paddleboats and swan shaped boats can be hired by the half-hour to take on the pond if you wish. Cost is 600-700 yen.

Address: 5-20 Uenokoen, Taito. Tokyo.
Hours: 24 hours.
Closest Station: Ueno Station, Park Exit.
Admission: Free.

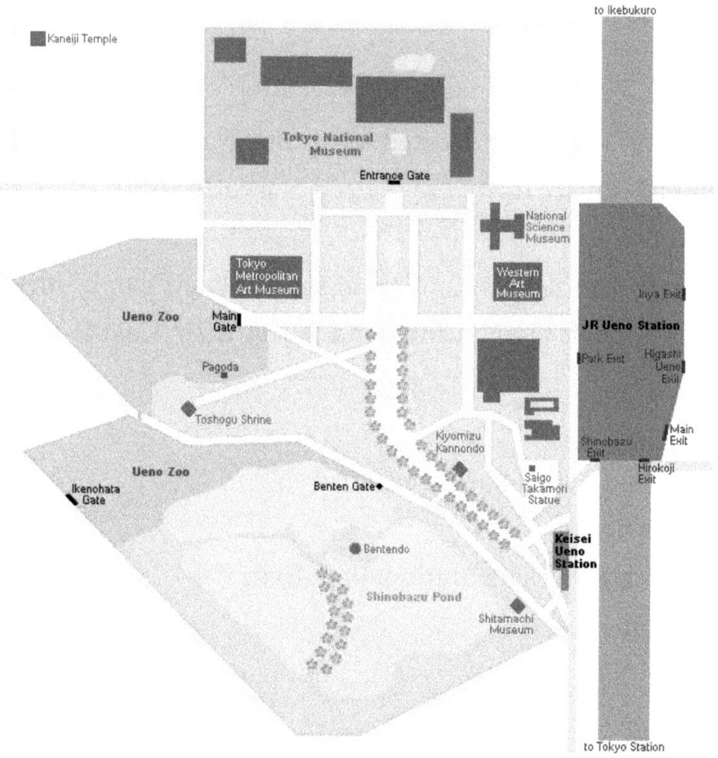

Ueno Park map

National Museum of Nature and Science/Tokyo Science Museum

Located in the northeast corner of Ueno Park. There are two galleries, the Japan Gallery, and Global Gallery. Exhibits include a statue of the famous Japanese Akita dog Hachiko, nature, organisms and people of Japan, the science of the earth and mammals. Descriptions are available in Japanese, English, Chinese and Korean.

The museum also holds a 360 degrees theatre where you stand on a bridge surrounded on all sides by a sphere of video and sound creating a 3D sensation.

There is a museum shop located in the Japan Gallery B1F and restaurant located on the Global Gallery Mezzanine level M2F open 10 am–5 pm Tuesday-Thursday. Friday and Saturday 10-8 pm.

https://www.kahaku.go.jp/english/

Address: 7-20 Ueno Park, Taito-Ku, Tokyo.
Hours: 9:00-17:00. Tue-Thur. 9.00- 20.00 Fri and Sat. Closed on Mondays.
Closest Station: Ueno Station.
Admission: 620-yen adults, Free for High school & younger.

Tokyo National Art Museum

Tokyo National Museum entrance

The National Art Museum in Tokyo is the largest in Japan. There are several buildings, each with its' own collection. The art within the museum focuses on ancient and medieval Japanese and Asian art in general and includes paintings, sculptures, calligraphy, and archeology. The collection has over 110'000 objects, many of them being Japanese National treasures (www.tnm.jp, 2020).

There is a museum shop located in the main building (first floor) and Main Gate Plaza. The Museum Shop sells a variety of items including t-shirts, stationery, bookmarks, prints, postcards, and traditional Japanese crafts such as ceramics and lacquerware. There is also a small section of English language publications about Japanese art.

There are two restaurants and a café selling food and beverages.

https://www.tnm.jp/?lang=en

TIPS

Tickets can be bought online from the Art Gallery's website. Audio guides for the regular exhibition in English, Japanese, Chinese and Korean can be hired from the main gate plaza for 500 yen. There is a limited supply.

Free WIFI is available throughout the museum *"TNM_Free_Wi-Fi."*

Note that photography, eating, drinking, and smoking are not allowed within the exhibition areas.

Address: 13-9 Ueno Park, Taito-Ku, Tokyo.
Hours: 9.30-5 pm Tuesday to Thursday. Open until 9pm on Friday and Saturdays. Closed Mondays.
Closest Station: A 10-minute walk from Ueno Station.
Admission: Adults 620-yen, University students 410-yen. Children under 18 free. Special exhibitions may require an extra fee.

Tokyo Metropolitan Museum of Art

This museum displays all types of art in its six galleries from famous artists to new artists. There isn't a permanent collection, but multiple temporary exhibitions by various art groups that change regularly.
The museum has a shop on the lower basement floor and a café on both the first and second floors. A quiet lounge area is available for use on the 1st floor.

TIPS

As the art on display is always changing, you can look up their website to see if the current art on display suits your interests before you go.

This is a popular art museum and can get busy, especially in the evenings and on the weekends. Arrive early and go on a weekday to avoid the crowds.

https://www.tobikan.jp/en/
Address: 8-36 Ueno-Park Taito-Ku.
Hours: 9:30 to 17:30 Tuesday-Thursday, Saturday, and Sunday. 9.30-8 pm Fridays. Closed Mondays.
Closest Station: A 7-minute walk Ueno JR Station, Park Exit. Or a 10-minute walk Ginza Metro Line, Hibiya Line.
Admission: Some of the exhibits are free; others require an admission fee.

Eastern Tokyo

Asakusa

Senso-Ji Temple and the Nakamise shopping markets

Senso-Ji is the oldest Buddhist temple in Tokyo and one of the most popular areas for visitors to Tokyo, so the area can get quite busy. I really loved the rich red and gold colours of the wooden temple and the Shinto shrine.

To get to the temple, you can pass through the Kaminarimon or "Thunder Gate". This imposing Buddhist structure features a huge paper lantern dramatically painted in vivid red and black colours to suggest thunderclouds and lightning and makes a great photo.

After visiting the temple, the markets are a great place to walk around and absorb the traditional atmosphere, watch Japanese snacks being made by hand (and try them!) and buy some cute presents to take home, such as colourful Japanese sweets (Wagashi) and hand fans.

Kaminarimon Gate at Senso-Ji Temple

TIP

For a donation of 100-yen, visitors can have your "fortune told". After paying your money, you choose one of the long metal containers, shake a labelled stick free from the container and read the corresponding fortune written on paper from one of the drawers. If you happen to get an unlucky fortune you can tie the "fortune" to a nearby wire (you will see others tied there) to remove the bad luck.

Buying a fortune

http://www.sensojitemple.com/

Address: 1-20 Asakusa, Taito City, Tokyo.

Hours: Senso-ji Temple 6 am-5 pm. Asakusa Shrine, open 24 hours.

Nakamise markets usually 9 am-7 pm depending on individual stalls.

Closest Station: Asakusa Station.

Admission: Free.

Hanayashiki amusement park

We stumbled upon this park after visiting the Senso-ji Temple in Asakusa. It is the oldest park in Japan having first opened in 1853. The park is quite small and has a retro feel compared to other parks such as Disney, however, we had a lot of fun here, and it wasn't too busy, which was a bonus.

Apart from rides and games there is also a Ninja school where they teach you swordplay, escape techniques and martial arts. The course runs for one hour and is more fun than serious so bring your sense of humour.

There is also a palm reading machine where you can have your fortune read and printed on a little paper ticket for 100 yen. The fortune is written in both Japanese and English.

https://www.hanayashiki.net/en

Address: 2-28-1 Asakusa, Taito City, Tokyo.
Hours: 10 am-6 pm.
Closest Station: Tokyo Metro Ginza Line / Toei Subway Asakusa Line / Tobu Sky Tree Line, 5 minutes on foot from Asakusa Station.
Admission: Adults-13 years, 1000-yen, 7 to 12-year-old, 500-yen. Children under 6 free. Single ride ticket 100-yen, coupon book (11 tickets) 1000-yen.

Tokyo Sky Tree.

At 634 metres, the Tokyo Sky Tree is the tallest structure in Japan and the world's highest free-standing broadcasting tower. There are several levels, including the Tembo observation deck, which is 350 meters above the ground and has amazing 360-degree panoramic views over Tokyo. My husband suffers from Vertigo and was not a fan of going close to the windows! There is also an even higher level at 450 meters from the ground called the Tembo Galleria. We didn't actually go up to this level; however, I'm sure it would have been even more spectacular!

The Sky Tree has a sit-down Café on the Tembo Deck floor 340, a stand selling ice cream and drinks on the Tembo Deck floor 350 and the Samurai Restaurant located on the Tembo Deck 345. The restaurant is 345 meters from the ground and has magnificent views over Tokyo. The cafes are open 8 am-9.30 pm and the restaurant is open 11 am-11 pm.

There are shops selling Sky Tree souvenirs on the 1st, 5th and Tembo Deck floor 345.

TIPS

If you want to skip the lines to the observation deck on level 350 there is a *Sky Tree Fast Pass* available for international visitors. The Fast Pass is available from the counter on the 4th floor west entrance. You must have your passport with you to purchase.

There are nursing rooms available on the first and 4th floor behind the ticket counters.
Coin-operated lockers are available, also foreign currency exchange machines if you need to convert cash into yen.
Free Wi-Fi is available in the tower *TOBU_Free_Wi-Fi*

http://www.tokyo-skytree.jp/en/

Address: 1-1-2 Oshiage, Sumida City, Tokyo.
Hours: 8 am-10 pm.
Closest Station: Tokyo Sky Tree Station.
Admission:
Combo ticket floor 350 and 450. Adults, 3100-yen weekdays, 3400-yen Sat and Sun.
Fast Pass ticket
Floor 350 only, adults and children over 12, 3200-yen. Children 6-11 years, 1600-yen.
Floor 350 and 450 combo, adults, and children over 12, 4200-yen. Children 6-11 years, 2100-yen.

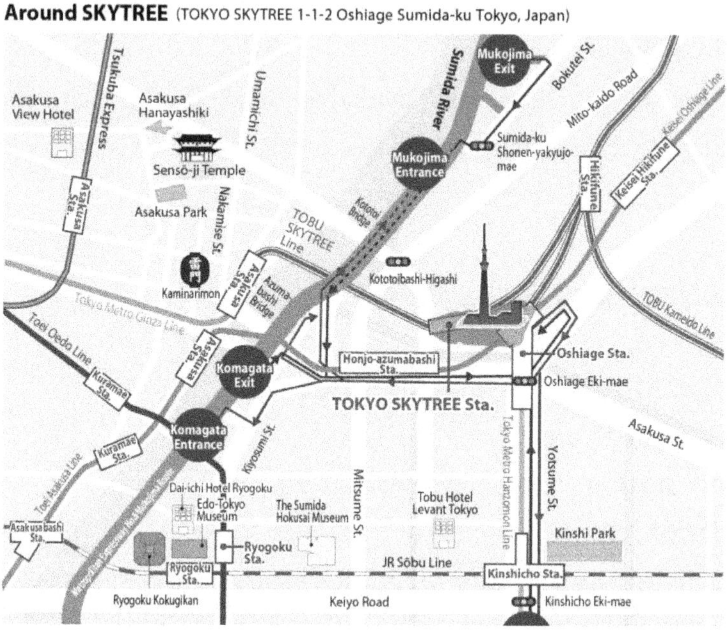

Around Sky Tree

Western Tokyo

Western Tokyo consists of the very popular prefectures of Shinjuku, Harajuku, and Shibuya. If you are after shopping, gardens, and interesting food, you'll find it here!

Shinjuku

Shinjuku is the commuting capital of Tokyo and contains the busiest train station in the world, (we got lost there several times!). This district contains the most skyscrapers in Tokyo and is full of neon signs which is why it is often used in filming movies such as Ghost in a Shell, Tokyo Drift and Lost in Translation.

We visited several parks as well as interesting museums and attractions in the area.

One of the pathways in the Shinjuku Gyoen Gardens

Shinjuku Gyoen National Gardens

This is a beautiful park with grassy lawns, serene lakes and pagodas offering a tranquil break from the frenzy of the city around it. We easily spent a couple of hours just strolling the grounds. There are more than 20,000 trees in the park with three distinct garden styles: English, French and Traditional Japanese. We went in the autumn when the leaves on the trees were beautiful shades of orange and yellow. It was a lovely way to get back to nature, rest our feet and take a break from shopping and site seeing!

Shinjuku Gyoen National Gardens

There were beautiful pagodas overlooking a lake which made lovely photographs and bridges with huge orange and white Koi fish swimming below. It was a really tranquil and peaceful spot to take in a bit of nature for a while. There is an information centre, a kiosk selling drinks and snacks and a teahouse in the gardens. Coin-operated lockers are available at the ticket office next to the entrance gate, sml/med 300-yen, large 500-yen.

Address: 11 Naitōmachi, Shinjuku City, Tokyo.
Hours: 9 am -6 pm. Closed Mondays.
Admission: Adults 500-yen. Children under 15-years old free.

KitKat Chocolatier Shinjuku

We stumbled across this store when looking around the Takashimaya Department store in Shinjuku. If you're a fan of KitKat chocolate and want to try something a little different, you'll find it here. The store is quite small; however, they have a large variety of KitKat chocolates in very different flavours than you will find at home. There are also displays of favourite flavours and samples to try. When we were there the flavours included strawberry, café latte, matcha (green tea) Sakura (cherry blossom), Sake, sweet potato, red apple, cheesecake, and tiramisu. The chocolate bars are boxed in gift packages and make an interesting souvenir to take home.

All kinds of Kit Kat chocolate flavours.

TIP The prices in this store are a little expensive, and unless you are looking for an exclusive flavour or nicely packaged gift, some of the flavours can also be purchased in packs from convenience stores and Don Quixote stores for a cheaper price.

There are also branches in Ginza and Ikebukuro.

Address: Basement level 1, Takashimaya Department store. 5-24-2 Sendagaya, Shinjuku. Tokyo.

Hours: 10 am-8 pm.

Closest Station: Shinjuku Station.

Samurai Museum

This small, interesting museum is situated in the Kabukicho district of Shinjuku where they give visitors a better understanding of Samurai culture, including how they fought, who they were, what they believed.

On the first floor, you will find the information desk, gift shop and armour exhibition in the Samurai Gallery. On the second floor are Samurai Katana swords and other weapons, an exhibition of Samurai history and Samurai costumes. There is also a photo area where you can take photographs in a samurai helmet (kabuto) and battle coat (jinbaori), there are also kimonos, fans, and parasols.

Samurai Museum Shinjuku

All visitors tour with a guide (English) who gives a lively presentation of about one hour on the Samurai lives and their history. You may then wander through the exhibits at your own pace. It concludes with a Samurai fight and opportunities to dress-up in Samurai costumes, or kimono.

The museum holds a free sword show which runs for about 15 minutes four times a day at 2 pm, 3 pm, 4 pm and 5 pm.

There are also extra activities available at the museum and include a Calligraphy Lesson (one hour), Japanese Sword Lecture (one hour) and Samurai Live Music Show (one hour). These all need to be reserved. This can be done at the museum (subject to availability) or online on their website.

TIPS

Make sure you hold onto your museum entry ticket as it gives you free access to the sword show.

https://www.samuraimuseum.jp/en/experience/index.html
Address: 1st floor Eiwa Dairoku Building, 2-25-6 Kabukicho, Shinjuku. Tokyo.
Hours: 10.30 am-9 pm Sunday-Friday. 10.30-8 pm Saturday.
Closest Station: 8-minute walk from Shinjuku Station on the JR Yamanote Line.
Admission: Adults 1900-yen, Children under twelve 800-yen. Children under three years are free.

Kani Doraku Crab Restaurant

The Kani Doraku Crab Restaurant has several locations throughout Japan. The one in Shinjuku has a giant moving crab out the front and as you probably guessed, serves a huge range of crab dishes.

There are many crab dishes to choose from, and you can either order dishes individually or choose a set menu. The meals were a little expensive; however, the food was delicious, so well worth it.

You will be asked to remove your shoes before eating and seating is at a low table with space for your legs or you may sit crossed legged.

TIPS

You will most likely need to book as the restaurant is very popular. Reservations can be made at the restaurant or online.

Note If booking online, the Tokyo branch of Kani Doraku is located under the Kanto region.

There are smoking and non-smoking areas so specify which you would prefer when making your booking.

http://douraku.co.jp.e.at.hp.transer.com/

Address: 3-27-10 Shinjuku. Level 4 Musashino Building, Shinjuku, Tokyo.

Hours: 11.30 am- 11 pm.

Nearest Station: Shinjuku Station or Shinjuku Sanchome.

Kani Doraku Restaurant in Shinjuku

Tokyo Metropolitan Government Building Observatory

This is well worth seeing as from the Observation deck of the Metropolitan Government building (the tallest building in Shinjuku) you can get an amazing view of Tokyo from 202 meters above the ground and it's free! There is a 360-degree view, and on a clear day you can see all the way to Mt Fuji.

Tokyo Metropolitan Government Buildings

TIPS

To access the observation deck, take the Observatory elevator from the 1st floor of main building number one to the 45th floor. There is usually a queue for the elevator; however, it moves quite quickly.

The South Observation Deck is closed on the first and third Tuesday of every month. The North Observation Deck is closed on the second and fourth Monday of every month.

On the 45th floor, there is a small café selling drinks, snacks, and souvenirs, plus a piano for visitors to play songs on!

If you are interested in the Olympic and Paralympic Games to be held in Tokyo in 2020, there is a display of the flags and further information about the games on the 2nd floor of the TMG building number one. Open 9.30 am- 6.45 pm.

There is a tourist information centre located on the 1st floor of TMG building number one. Which has maps and general information on Tokyo and Japan in general. Open 9.30 am-6.30 pm.

If you are craving coffee, there is a Tully's Coffee shop on the 2nd floor of the TMG building number 2. Open 8 am-6 pm

If you want to purchase takeaway food and drinks, there is a convenience store called Famima!! located on the 1st floor of the TMG building number 2. Open 7 am-9 pm.

http://www.yokoso.metro.tokyo.jp/en/tenbou/index.html

Address: 2-8-1 Nishi-Shinjuku, Shinjuku 160-0023, Tokyo.
Hours: 9.30-11 pm.
Closest Station: 10-minute walk Shinjuku Station, West Exit. Tochomae Station, Toei Oedo subway line.
Admission: Free.

Harajuku

Harajuku Takeshita Dori (shopping street)

Only a short distance from Shibuya is Harajuku's Takeshita Dori. A bustling narrow street crammed with fast food shops, cafes, clothes retailers, and quirky shops. Even if you don't plan on buying anything, this is a great place to people watch and look through the interesting stores. Be prepared, it can get very busy in the evenings and on the weekends.

The start of Takeshita Dori

Takeshita Dori has many stalls serving fresh crepes filled with fruit and cream, monster ice cream cones, giant fairy floss, coloured bubble teas, colourful candies, and cute sweets. Some examples include:

Totti Candy Factory

Selling colourful sweets, cake pops and giant rainbow fairy floss/ cotton candies like the Unicorn multi coloured cotton candy. Get ready for a sugar rush! Two girls in maid costumes and cat ears make cotton candy as you wait.

For the rainbow versions, they pour in the different colours one by one. It's quite cool to watch. The store is very popular, and there is usually at least a 15-minute wait.

Address: RYU apartment 2nd floor, 1-16-5 Jingumae, Shibuya, Tokyo.
Approximately halfway down Takeshita Street in Harajuku.
Hours: 10.30-8 pm Monday–Friday. 9.30-8 pm Saturday and Sunday.
Closest Station: JR Harajuku Station or Tokyo Metro Meiji Jingumae Station.
Cost: 300 to 900-yen.

Dobutsuen

The Zoo Ice Cream Shop, where you can choose your preferred ice cream animal from elephants, koalas, panda bears, tigers or pigs. Each animal has a different flavour of ice-cream and decoration. For example, the Koala has Oreo biscuits for ears, and the pig has a marshmallow for a nose. They are extremely cute, and your kids will love them. The storefront is set up to look just like a vending machine.

Very cute animal ice creams from Dobutsen

Address: 3-20-7 Jingumae, Shibuya, Tokyo.
Hours: 11 am-7 pm.**Closest Station:** JR Harajuku Station
Cost: 500-yen per ice-cream.

Le Shinier

Selling rainbow coloured grilled cheese sandwiches and multi-coloured ice-cream!

TIP It is considered rude to walk and eat, so stand outside the store you bought your ice-cream or fairy floss/cotton candy from to eat or find a quiet place to sit if you can. The store will usually take your candy stick from you when you have finished. The start of Takeshita Street is right outside Harajuku Station. You can get to Harajuku on the train on either the JR Yamanote Line to Harajuku Station, or the Tokyo Metro Chiyoda Line to Meiji-jingu Mae with is then a 5-minute walk to Harajuku.

Address: 1st floor, 1-7-10 Jingumae, Shibuya-ku, Tokyo.
Hours: 11 am-6 pm Monday-Friday. 10.30 am-7 pm Saturday and Sunday.
Closest Station: JR Harajuku Station or Tokyo Metro Meiji Jingumae Station.

Rainbow sandwich from Le Shinier

Marion Crepes serving both savoury and sweet crepes, this is one of Japans' oldest crepe shops. My favourite is the strawberry and whipped cream crepe. There is a display case with all the types of crepes available written in both Japanese and English.

TIP

There can be a queue depending on whether it is a weekend or the time of day. My suggestion is to walk past and see how long the line is first, and if it is very long, do some shopping or browse the streets before heading back. We went during the week when the crowds were less and didn't have to wait very long at all.

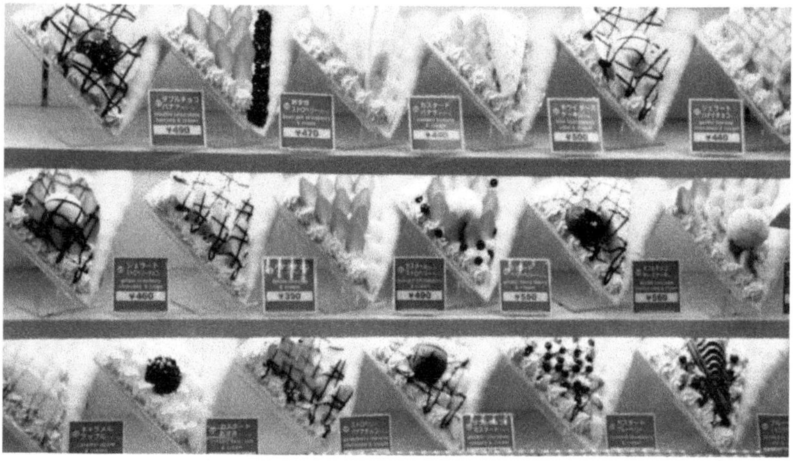

Huge variety of crepes in Harajuku

Address: 1-6-15 Jingumae Shibuya, Tokyo.
Closest Station: JR Harajuku Station or Tokyo Metro Meiji Jingumae Station.

Kiddyland

If you are looking for toys, plushies and collectables then you will want to pay a visit to Kiddyland which is not just for kids!

Kiddyland is located in Omotesando Street, Harajuku. This five-story toy emporium first opened in 1950 and contains plushies, Lego, Hello Kitty, Pikachu, Totoro, Rirakkuma, collectables and a whole lot more. Expect to spend a couple of hours here with your children!

https://www.kiddyland.co.jp/harajuku/

Address: 4-31-10 Jingumae, Shibuya. Tokyo.
Hours: Mon -Fri 11-9 pm, Sat and Sun 10.30 am-9 pm.
Closest Station: Shibuya Station.
Admission: Free.

Shibuya

Shibuya is one of the liveliest and trendiest places in Tokyo, and you will see a lot of younger people walking around, shopping, having dinner and going to Karaoke or clubs here.

TIPS

Shibuya and Harajuku are within walking distance of each other, and you may not even realise you have crossed from one prefecture to the other.

Shibuya's streets can be quite confusing so in order to not get lost, stick to where you can see the neon lights and signs, and you will be close to Shibuya Station.

The main train station is located at the lowest spot in Shibuya, so if you get lost, as long as you are on a descending street, it should lead you back to the station.

Shibuya Crossing

Great for that Instagram photo! The intersection or crossing at Shibuya is amazing to watch. With each light change, hundreds of people calmly cross the intersection at once in multiple directions like a large, carefully choreographed flash mob. The busiest time is after 5 pm Monday to Friday.

Shibuya crossing at a quiet time

TIP

We found the best place to watch people crossing was from the second floor of Starbucks, which is located directly opposite the crossing.

Centre Gai

Centre Gai is the pedestrian street that begins on the other side of Shibuya crossing (see above). It is filled with fashion stores, interesting eateries, and game centres. It is one of the liveliest streets in the area, particularly in the evenings and at the weekends.

TIP

If you don't like the crowds, plan on visiting Centre Gai during the week rather than on the weekend and during the day when it is less crowded.

Karaoke

Karaoke is a very popular pastime, where you can hire your own private room to sing and dance to your heart's content. Food and drinks can also be ordered and brought to your room and songs can be chosen in either English or Japanese. Some examples of Karaoke establishments in Tokyo are:

Karaoke Kan

Address: 30-8 Udagawacho, Shibuya, Tokyo.
Hours: 11 am – 4 pm.
Nearest Station: Shibuya Station, Hachiko Exit.
Admission: pay by the hour.

Karaoke no Tetsujin Shimbashi SL Hiroba

Address: 2-9-9 Shinbashi, Minato, Tokyo.

Hours: 12 pm- 6 am.

Nearest Station: Shinbashi Station.

Admission: The price is by the hour and depends upon whether you visit during the day or evening and whether you want a drinks package (alcoholic or non-alcoholic) included.

Karaoke No Tetsujin Ginza

Address: 5-9-11 Ginza Midori building, 5th floor. Chuo, Tokyo.

Hours: Saturday and Sunday 11am-6 am. Monday to Friday 12 pm-6 am.

Nearest Station: Tokyo Metro Ginza Station, A3 Exit.

Admission: The price depends upon daytime or night-time visit and food/drinks you purchase.

Yoyogi Park and Meiji Shrine

This is a large park with lots of tall trees and a great place to visit and unwind. You can take a picnic with you, or just enjoy a walk in the park and get back to nature. Lots of benches are available around the park and are free to use.

There are several entrances to the park, with the main entrance lined with trees and temporary stalls selling all sorts of wares and food.

Meiji Shrine is also located near the park, and we are lucky to witness a traditional Shinto wedding being held at the time we visited. It is a lovely experience, and we saw a lot of cute children dressed in their traditional kimonos.

Beautiful autumn leaves at Yoyogi Park

TIP

If you want to go on a bike ride, there are bicycles available to rent for adults, children and tandem. It's a great way to see more of the park for a very reasonable price. To rent a bike, you first purchase a voucher from the bicycle vending machine, fill out the information on the form, then take the form to the rental counter.

Costs for bike hire for an hour are 210-yen for an adult bike, 100-yen for a children's bike and 210-yen for a tandem bike. Open 9 am to 4 pm. Closed on Mondays.

https://www.tokyo-park.or.jp/park/format/map039.html

Address: 2-1 Yoyogi Kamizonocho, Shibuya Tokyo.
Hours: open 24 hours.
Closest Station: There are several entrances to the park. The closest station to the main entrance is Harajuku.
Admission: Free.

Hachiko Statue

Located in Shibuya directly outside the Shibuya subway station. First built in the 1930s in honour of a dog named Hachiko who waited at the station every day for his master to return from work. Even after his master passed away, Hachiko returned to the station at the same time each day for the next nine years to faithfully wait in vain for his master. Eventually, Hachiko himself also passed away. The poignant story of Hachiko is well-known in Japanese culture, and the statue commemorates both Hachiko and the values of traditional family loyalty he represents. Hachiko has also had a Hollywood movie made after him (it's a tearjerker!)

Hachiko

Photobooths Purikura/ Print Club

Both my daughters (and myself if I am honest!) love having fun with these photobooths. Yes, you can take funny photos of yourself, but you can also decorate them on screen before printing them out on take-home photo strips. It is a lot of fun and not too expensive. Cost is usually 300-400 yen.
The photos do tend to alter your face by making your eyes larger and rounder like a doll's, however, this is part of the fun.

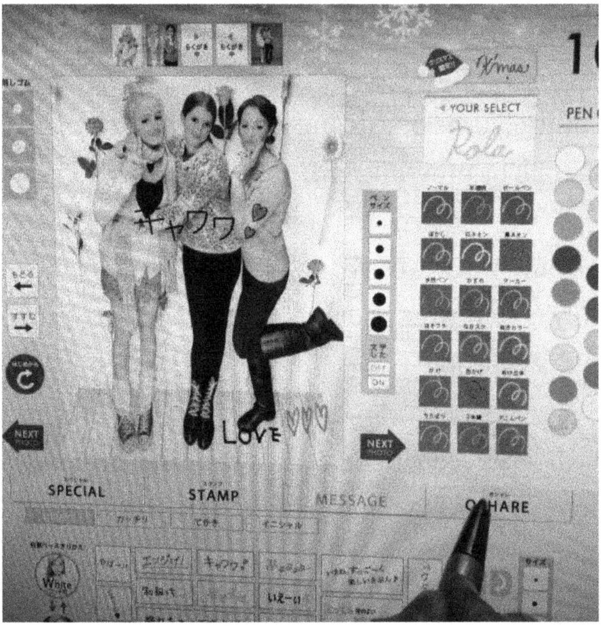

Photo editing in Purikura

TIPS

In the editing booth, you can choose from multiple layout designs for your print and customize each individual photo. You can write or draw on them, for example, cat whiskers, stick stamps such as love hearts or crowns, add makeup touches like blush, eyelashes, etc. The editing options are usually in Japanese, however, so it can be a little confusing. We just tapped around with the stylus to figure out which tab we were on e.g. draw/write, stamp, etc. and had fun with it. And we had a laugh at the finish!

There is a limited time on editing your photos, or you can choose not to edit at all by pressing end.

The booths only work well for four or less people at once. They are generally not very big booths, and the sensors cannot pick up more than a few people.

Most of the booths seem to be geared towards females; however, I did see some males having fun with them too.

A couple of examples of Purikura booths are:

Moreru Mignon this Purikura shop is very cute. There are giant pastel cakes and doughnuts decorating the shop with mirrors for a touch-up before your photos!
2nd basement floor (BF) of the Shibuya 109 Mall. They're open from 10am until 9pm daily. Cost is 500-yen and there is an English instruction sheet.

Purikura Land NOA this purikura centre has a lot of booths and is very popular. It is located in Harajuku off Takeshima Street. You need to go down the stairs to access it. Basement level 1, 1-17-5 Jingumae Shibuya.

Purikura no Mecca first floor, 29-1 Udagawacho, Shibuya City. Tokyo.

Purikuri waiting area at Moreru Mignon

Kipposhi (coloured noodles)

Small ramen restaurant where the noodles and broth are light pink, blue, or green in colour! Chicken slices are served rather than the traditional pork, and the broth is lighter in flavour than traditional ramen.

Blue Ramen

TIP

Kipposhi is not far from Yoyogi park, the Sky tree and Hachiko statue. There is also a large Don Quixote store which is good for souvenirs nearby.

Address: 1-11-5 Dainesu-Ichibankan 102, Shibuya. Tokyo.
Hours: 11.30-3 pm lunch. 6-9.30 Dinner. Closed Wednesdays.
Closest Station: Shibuya Station.

Tama

Sanrio Puroland (Hello Kitty theme park)

This is a very cute indoor amusement park for fans of Hello Kitty, My Melody, Gudetama and other SanRio characters. The park has parades and shows featuring Hello Kitty and other characters, games and rides, shops and restaurants spread over 4 floors.

The shops include:
My Melody
Kiki and Lala
Cinnamoroll
Gudetama
Sweet Shop
Hello Kitty

The restaurants are all character-themed and include:
The Character food court with pasta and curry modelled on SanRio characters.
Cinnamoroll Dream Café which is a cute dessert shop.
The Sweet Parlour serves ice-cream and drinks, including soft drinks and beer!

Sanrio Rainbow World is a very colourful rainbow-themed restaurant serving pasta, roast beef over rice and other brightly coloured foods.

TIPS

Like all other theme parks, this one can become extremely busy. I recommend buying your tickets online. Tickets can usually be bought a few days before.

The trip to Tama town takes about 30 mins by train from Shinjuku Station, so leave early and give yourself plenty of time to get there.

https://en.puroland.jp/homeen/ticket_en/

Tama-Center, the city of Hello Kitty, is about 30 minutes by train from Shinjuku Station and 60 minutes from Tokyo Station.

Address: 1-31 Ochiai, Tama, Tokyo.
Hours: Open 9.30-5 pm.
Closest Station: Odakyu Tama Centre Station 30 minutes from Shinjuku Station.
Admission: Adults (17 and older) 3500-yen, children 2500-yen.

Nakano

Nakano Broadway

This covered shopping arcade is filled with interesting shops and eateries and a great place for fans of Anime and Manga. There are also several stores selling second-hand clothing and collectable toys and dolls.

Nakano Broadway shopping arcade

TIPS

Walk straight ahead from the Nakano train station (north Exit), and you will come to the shopping arcade. At the ends of the arcade, you will find Akihabara type stores such as Mandarake which are good for gaming, anime, and manga (comic book) products.

If you're craving some fast-food Western style, there is a MacDonalds located in this mall!

The second floor is only accessible by the stairs.
Address: 5-52-15 Nakano, Nakano, Tokyo.
Hours: Depends on each shop/restaurant.
Closest Station: Nakano Station, North Exit. Chuo line.
Admission: Free.

Dolls for sale in Nakano Broadway

Manga Drawing school

This is a unique concept where visitors can learn to draw Manga (Japanese cartoons) from a Japanese Manga artist. The Lessons are conducted in English by artist Nao Yazawa. All equipment is supplied, and no experience is necessary.

There are mini-courses, standard courses and longer courses available (see the Manga Drawing School's website for more details.) Standard lessons are two hours long.

TIPS

To book a class fill in the contact form on their website and they will email you back.

Directions on how to get to the classroom will be emailed to you after you make your booking.

The school is not far from the Nakano Broadway Shopping Arcade, so you can stop for a drink, ice cream, snack, or shopping on your way home. The store Mandarake has a large store selling new and used Manga.

https://english.nakanomangaschool.jp/

Address: 2-7-13 Arai Nangoku Building, second floor. Nakano, Tokyo.

Hours: Mon.- Fri. 10:00-12:00, 13:00-15:00, 16:00 - 18:00 /17:30-19:30 or 18:30-20:30.

Closest Station: 10-minute walk from Nakano Station, North Exit. Chuo line.
Admission: Depends on class type and how many students are attending. For example, a standard 2-hour class costs 13000 yen for a private lesson, 8000 yen for 2-4 people. See website for further details.

Daily Chiko Mega ice cream

If you like ice cream, you'll enjoy visiting Daily Chiro located in the Nakano Broadway Shopping complex. They have a huge range of flavours some which you might not have tried before. When we were there, the flavours included vanilla, chocolate, strawberry, coffee, banana, grape, matcha (green tea) and ramune (lemonade). The large size is eight layers tall so you might want to share this one!
The price depends on whether you want a cone or cup and the size. A small cone (1-2 flavours) is 280-yen. A medium cone (3-4 flavours) is 380-yen and a large (5-8 flavours) is 550-yen.

Eight flavour ice cream from Daily Chiro

TIPS

You'll need to eat your ice cream while you are at the ice cream stand as the Japanese do not eat and walk. There aren't any tables and chairs, so just stand out in front of the shop and enjoy your treat.

Be careful when eating the large size as it can topple, and no refills are given.

Address: B1F 5-52-15 Nakano Broadway. Tokyo. Open 10-8.30pm

Closest Station: Nakano Station, North Exit, Chuo line.

Kasugacho

Warner Bros Studio Tour – The Making of Harry Potter

The new Harry Potter Studio Tour is great fun if you are a fan of Harry Potter or the Fantastic Beasts series. Located in Nerima Kasugacho the studio can be accessed by train from Tokyo on the Ikebukuro station or Metro Oedo line.

Tickets need to be purchased online from their website in advance. Tickets - Warner Bros. Studio Tour Tokyo - The Making of Harry Potter (wbstudiotour.jp)

The studio has lots of exhibits from the Harry Potter series including costumes, props, special effects, and models.
Sets include Diagon Ally, platform three quarters, the Forbidden Forrest (my favourite), the great hall and fantastic beasts.
There is a souvenir shop called the Potter shop and a café selling sweets and butter beer.

4

Costume display at Harry Potter studio.

Chapter Seven

Day trips from Tokyo

There are many other interesting places to visit and where you go depends upon how much time you have for your holiday and your own interests. I have listed below several interesting places that can be seen as a day trip from Tokyo.

Mt Fuji and Hakone

Mount Fuji is the largest mountain in Japan and can be seen from Tokyo on a clear day. If you want to take a closer look at the mountain, there are several ways to get there on a day trip.

TIPS There is a lot to see in this location, and unless you are staying for a few days in the area, a good way to see a bit of everything is to join an organised day tour. The hotel you are staying at should be able to organise one for you, or a local travel agent.

Check the weather before you leave Tokyo, if it is going to be rainy or cloudy you won't see Mt Fuji.

Mt Fuji

Mt Fuji Panoramic Ropeway

This is a great way to enjoy the view of Mt. Fuji from up the hill by a cable car on a sunny day. If it is cloudy, you won't see much of Mt Fuji, however, you will still have a view to the lakes below. To reach the cable car, the walk from the Kawaguchiko Station takes approximately 15-minutes.

TIPS

There is a shop at the top of the ropeway selling merchandise and snacks such as Dango if you feel the need.

The cable car can be very cramped with a lot of people, so if you feel like a walk, you can also walk to the top to see the view and enjoy some nature on the way. The walk takes about 40 minutes. Note that sometimes the cable car is closed if the weather is too windy; however, you are still permitted to walk to the top.

After purchasing your ticket, you will be given a number for the ropeway, don't wander too far or you will lose your spot!

Tickets can also be purchased in combination with a cruise on Lake Kawaguchi.
For more information, see the website below.

https://www.mtfujiropeway.jp/en/

Address: 1163-1 Azagawa, Fujikawaguchiko-machi, Minamitsuru.Yamanashi.
Hours: 9am-5pm.
Nearest Station: JR Chuo Limited express to Otsuki Station, then Fuikyu Railway to Kawaguchiko Station.
You can also catch an Expressway bus from Tokyo Station to Kawaguchiko Station (approx. 2 hours). Seats for the bus need to be reserved in advance. The bus is the quickest way there.
Admission: Ropeway, round-trip 900-yen adult, 450-yen children. One-way trip, 500-yen adult, 250-yen children. Children under 6-years old travel free with an adult.
Cruise/ Ropeway combo 1600-yen adult and 800-yen child.

Mt Fuji 5th Station

If you want to get right up close to Mt Fuji, then take a visit to the 5th Station as it is right at the base of the mountain itself. Many people hike up to the top of Mt Fuji from here (4-6 hours), or you can follow the path a little way along if you don't want to go the whole way.

TIPS

There is a little souvenir shop that also sells drinks and snacks, plus there is a bathroom (cost is 100-yen).

There are several areas to get good views of Mt Fuji, the Japanese Alps and lake Kawaguchi. I found the best view from the little shrine hidden behind the shops.

If you or your children like collecting stamps or want to send a special postcard to their friends from Mt Fuji, visit the post office at the 5th Station as they sell special Mt Fuji stamps not available elsewhere.

Address: Narusawa-mura, Minamitsuru, Yamanashi.
Nearest Station: Mt Fuji 5th Station. You can catch the Fujikyuko express bus from Shinjuku, Tokyo to the Mt Fuji 5th Station. Seats need to be reserved in advance.
Hours: 12am-12pm.

View of Mt Fuji from 5th Station.

Hakone

The Hot springs town of Hakone is a popular holiday destination for the Japanese and tourists alike. There are many places to see in this area, and although it can be seen as a day trip, it is also worthwhile staying a few nights.

Hakone is easily reached from Tokyo on the Odakyu line from Shinjuku Station. Or the JR Tokaido line from Tokyo Station. The journey takes 90 minutes.

https://hakone-japan.com/

TIPS

If you have a JR Rail pass, use the Tokaido line Shinkansen and change trains at Odawara Station.

There is also a bus available from Shinjuku Station in Tokyo and takes approximately 2 hours. Seats need to be reserved in advance.

The *Hakone Free Pass* is worthwhile getting if you are planning on doing a few activities during your stay as it covers the cost of the cable car, Lake Ashinoko boat ride, Tozan Mountain railway etc. See the website for more details.
https://hakone-japan.com/plan-your-trip/getting-around/hakone-freepass/

Some of the things to do in Hakone include:

Visiting the hot springs.

Two examples are.
Tenzan A collection of hot spring pools, most of which are outdoors at the foot of a wooded slope. The bath house is a beautiful traditional Japanese style building. A short walk from Oku-Yumoto Iriguchi bus stop (bus line K).
Open 9:00 to 11 pm, Admission 1300-yen.

Hakone Kamon Multiple outdoor baths made of stone and wood including a sauna. You are also served a cup of green tea after the bath. To get there, take the short shuttle bus ride from Yumoto Station (100 yen).
Open 10.30-5 pm, Admission is 1800-yen. Overnight stay is also available.

Seeing Mt Fuji across from Lake Ashinoko while you take a boat ride.

Mount Fuji can be seen from Lake Ashinoko; however, clouds and poor visibility often block the view. Visibility tends to be better during the colder seasons of the year and in the early morning and late afternoon. Even if you cannot see Mount Fuji, the views from the lake are lovely, and you can take a boat (including a pirate ship!) around the lake for approximately 30 minutes. The cost is 1050-yen. The Hakone Free Pass included a free trip on the pirate ship.

Viewing the Hakone Shinto Shrine.

The main Shrine stands at the foot of Mount Hakone along the shores of Lake Ashi and the second shrine called Mototsumiya stands at the summit of Mount Komagatake. This shrine can be visited by the Hakone Komagatake Ropeway, or via hiking trails.

Visiting a museum such as the *Open-Air Museum* with sculptures and paintings or the *Pola Cosmetics Museum.*

Seeing Odawara Castle. The Castle was originally built in the 15th Century and is now a popular spot for cherry blossom viewing in Spring. The interior of the castle has exhibits on the history of the castle as well as displays of items such as armour and swords. Open from 9am-5pm, admission is 510-yen.

Taking the Hakone Ropeway (cable car) 30-minute ride which takes you from Souzan Station to the shore of Lake Ashinoko. 150-yen one way, or free with Hakone Free Pass.

Taking the Komagatake Ropeway (cable car). This ropeway leads from the shore of Lake Ashinoko to the peak of Mount Hakone. When visibility is good, there are panoramic views of Mount Fuji and Lake Ashinoko. The second Hakone Shrine Mototsumiya also stands here. A roundtrip is 1600-yen. Not covered by the Hakone Free Pass; however, a discount applies.

Taking a ride on the Hakone Tozan Mountain Train. This spectacular ride on Japan's oldest mountain train takes you through wooded valleys, over bridges and through tunnels. 410-yen one way, or free with Hakone Free Pass.

Fuji Q Highland

This is an amusement park located near the base of Mt Fuji in Fujiyoshida, Yamanashi. The Park houses several rollercoasters, as well as two haunted attractions, the Haunted Hospital, and the Despair Fortress, plus an Attack on titan ride, Naruto ride and Ferris wheel.
During winter there is an outdoor ice-skating rink and a snow play park.
The Park also has several special character areas such as Thomas Land, and a Naruto Shippuden Museum.

http://www.fujiq.jp/en/area/highland/

Address: Fuji-Q Highland 5-6-1 Niahihara, Fujiyoshida, Yamanashi.
Hours: 9 am-6 pm.
Closest Station: If travelling to Mt Fuji on the Fujiyu Line, get off at Fujikyu Highland **Station** (yes, the amusement park has its own station!).
Admission: Entrance is free then you pay per ride/attraction. 800 – 1500 yen per ride or purchase an all-day or half-day pass. Internet tickets are 6000-yen all day pass, 4000-yen half day pass. Priority tickets can also be purchased.

Thomas Land

Thomas land has a Thomas the Tank Engine theme from the popular television series. There are rides, games, mazes, and photo opportunities with life like Thomas characters, as well as Thomas restaurants and merchandise available. The rides are usually 400-500 yen. There are baby changing facilities in this area and a nursing room. Further information can be found on their website.

http://www.fujiq.jp/en/

Address: Fuji-Q Highland 5-6-1 Niahihara, Fujiyoshida, Yamanashi.
Hours: 9 am-5 pm.
Closest Station: If travelling to Mt Fuji on the Fujiyu Line, get off at Fujikyu Highland Station.
Admission: Entrance is free then you pay per ride/attraction or purchase an all-day or half-day pass. Internet tickets are 6000-yen all day pass, 4000-yen half-day pass. Priority tickets can also be purchased.

Naruto and Borto Fuji Hidden Leaf Village

This area of the theme park houses a Naruto Museum, arcade games, a photo area, merchandise shop, café, and restaurant. For more information on each area, see their website.

http://www.fujiq.jp/en/area/narutoboruto/

Address: Fuji-Q Highland 5-6-1 Niahihara, Fujiyoshida, Yamanashi.
Hours: 9 am-5 pm.
Closest Station: If travelling to Mt Fuji on the Fujiyu Line, get off at Fujikyu Highland Station.
Admission: Entrance is free then you pay per ride/attraction purchase an all-day or half-day pass. Internet tickets are 6000-yen all day pass, 4000-yen half-day pass. Priority tickets can also be purchased.

Studio Ghibli Museum

This very interesting museum dedicated to the work of Studio Ghibli is located in Mitaka, which is about 30 minutes by train from Shinjuku Station in Tokyo and makes a nice day trip. Our family are fans of the Studio Ghibli movies and artwork, we loved this museum.

Giant Robot at the Studio Ghibli Museum

The Ghibli Museum is filled with lots of interesting rooms, including a workroom showcasing sketches and ideas from past Ghibli films, such as *Spirited Away, Howl's Moving Castle and Ponyo*. Your entry ticket includes a short film in the theatre and a screen shot from one of the Ghibli movies to take home.

There is a souvenir shop and small café called The Straw Hat Café if you wish to purchase food/ drinks etc. Outside in the garden area stands a giant robot from the movie *Laputa Castle in the Sky*. To get to Mitaka, you need to catch the local train from Shinjuku Station in Tokyo.

TIPS

The museum is quite a distance from the train station on foot (approx. 15-20 minutes), so I suggest taking the "cat bus" to the museum and back for a small fee.

Tickets to the museum need to be purchased in advance. We got ours online, and they can be purchased up to 3 months in advance. They are also available through some travel agencies, such as JTB travel.

When you enter the museum, you will be given a slide. Take a close look at it, and you will see that it is a screenshot of one of the frames from a Ghibli film!

http://www.ghibli-museum.jp/en/

Address: 1-1-83 Shimorenjaku, Mitaka-shi.

Hours: 10 am-6 pm.

Closest Station: JR Mitaka Station. Take the JR Chuo Line, approximately 20 minutes from JR Shinjuku Station to get to Mitaka Station. Exit at South Exit.

Admission: Adults and children over 19, 1000-yen. Children 13-18 years old, 700-yen. Children 7-12 years old, 400-yen. Children 4-6 years old, 100-yen. Children under 4, free.

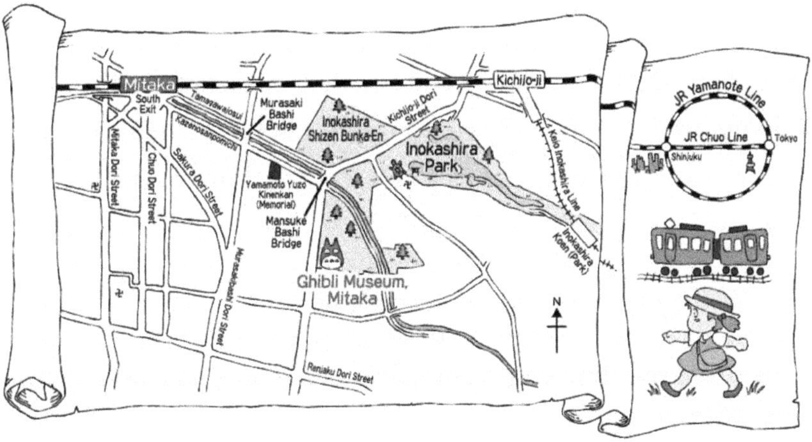

Map of how to get to the Studio Ghibli Museum

Yomiuriland Theme Park.

Yomiuriland Theme Park is both an amusement park and water park. This park is only 30 minutes by train from Shinjuku Station in Tokyo. The park has over 45 rides and includes a bungee jump, Bandit roller coaster which travels at 110 km per hour through a forest, an indoor fashion roller coaster, 5 swimming pools, 3 water slides and a Ferris Wheel with a view of Mt Fuji. There is also a sea lion show. Some of the rides do have height restrictions for safety reasons, and children must be accompanied by an adult.

Several restaurants and food stands are available in the park and include food such as curry rice, ramen, a soup kitchen, western food (burgers and fries), as well as popcorn, churros, and crepes.

TIPS

If you visit during the end of October to mid-February, the park holds a Jewellumination where the park is lit up at night with colourful changing lights for Christmas and the New Year.

If you visit during spring, the park's 1000 cherry blossoms may be out in flower where you can see them from the ground and from the air in the gondola.

From the Keio Yomiuriland or Yomiuriland-Mae Stations catch the Odakyu Bus (accepts Suica and Pasmo cards or 210-yen) or ride the gondola (Single 300-yen Return 500-yen) to the theme park.

If you plan on going on more than one ride and want to see the Sea Lion show, the day pass is worth getting as it gives you free entrance to the show plus unlimited rides.

There is free WIFI available at the entrance and in some of the restaurants.

Coin lockers are available.

English maps are available where you purchase your tickets.

Yomiuriland for Jewelillumination

http://www.yomiuriland.com/english/

Address: 4015 Yanokuchi Inagi.
Hours:10-9pm Monday-Wednesday. 10-8.30 pm Thursday-Saturday. 9.30-8.30 pm Sunday.
Closest Station: Keio Yomiuriland Station, Keio line from Shinjuku Station in Tokyo (platform 4). Yomiuriland-Mae Station, Odakyu line from Shinjuku Station in Tokyo.
Admission: 1800-yen 18 years and older. 1500-yen Juniors (13-18 years). 1000-yen child and preschool (4-13 years). This is an entrance only fee and does not include rides or attractions.

Day Pass: (includes entrance, rides, and sea lion show) 5500-yen 18 years and older. 4400-yen, 13-18 years old. 3900-yen, 6-13 years. 3400-yen 4-6 years old.
There are also night passes available if you plan on only going after 4pm.

Chapter Eight

Tokyo's best themed cafes

A fun thing to try is the themed café/restaurant. The cafes usually sell drinks and fun food often related to the café's theme. There are many different themed cafes, some allow photographs inside, some do not (if you are unsure just ask the wait staff), most sell related merchandise. Some of the of themed cafes we have been to are:

Shiro-Hige's Cream Puff Factory

Custard filled cream puff Totoro.

This very cute café selling delightfully tasty Studio Ghibli style Totoros is located in the Tolo Coffee and Bakery store. The filled Totoros make cute photographs and come in three different flavours, custard, chocolate, and caramel banana.

The puffs cost 500 yen and because of their popularity can sell out.

Address: 5 Chome-3-1 Daita, Setagaya City, Tokyo.
Hours: 10.30am-7pm closed on Tuesdays.
Closest Station: 2-minute walk to the north-east of Setagaya-Daita Station (Odakyu Line), or a 7-minute walk south-west of Shimo-Kitazawa Station (Odakyu Line, Keio-Inokashira Line).

Honey Toast Café

Though not a "theme" café" I just had to put this one in here as I had never been to a café dedicated to toast before!
The café serves fresh toast made from handmade bread. The bread inside the loaf is removed, soaked in honey and butter and baked crispy. Sounds very decadent and it tasted wonderful! There are varieties of food available at the cafe from French toast, regular honey toast, honey toast with various toppings and savoury items. Milkshakes and other drinks are also available.

TIPS

There is free WIFI and power charging available within the café, however, you will need a power converter to access this.

Reservations can be made online, or in store. If you are planning on going on a Saturday or Sunday, you will need to make reservations to ensure a table.

https://www.pasela.co.jp/shop/akiba_multi/honeytoastcafe/

Address: 1st floor Pasela Resorts Akihabara. 1-1-10 Sotokanda, Chiyoda Tokyo.

Hours: 9 am-10.30 pm.

Closest Station: 3-minute walk, Akihabara Station, Denkigai Exit. Or 3 to 5-minute walk, Subway Hibiya Line, Akihabara Station Exit.

Alice in a Fantasy Book (Alice in Wonderland Café)

My teenage daughters loved this very cute little restaurant located in Shinjuku with an Alice in Wonderland theme. The food and drinks are all related to Alice and her friends and are all very Kawaii (cute). The wait staff all dress in Alice in Wonderland attire, and the restaurant is decorated to match with red hearts, roses and playing cards everywhere. There are both alcoholic and nonalcoholic drinks available. Plastic versions of the food available to order are on display at the entrance of the restaurant. You will need to book for this restaurant as they are very busy.

One of the cute desserts in the Alice in Wonderland Restaurant

TIP

We found this restaurant difficult to find as it is located in the basement of a building tucked away in a corner. Ask your hotel to write the name of the restaurant and address in Japanese so you can easily ask/show to get directions.

Table reservations can be made online.
http://www.alice-restaurant.com/ehon/

Address: Basement floor 2. T-wing Building, 1-6-2 Kabukicho, Shinjuku, Tokyo.
Hours: Monday-Friday 17:00-23:30 Saturday and Sundays Lunch 11:30-15:00 Dinner 16:00-23:30.
Closest Station: 3-minute walk, JR Shinjuku Station, East Exit. Or 4 minutes' walk, Seibu Shinjuku Line, Seibu Shinjuku Station, South Exit.

Hello Kitty Café, Konguriyaki

The Hello Kitty Café Konguriyaki is located in the Diver City shopping complex in Odaiba and specialises in Hello Kitty themed pancakes, lattes and other Hello Kitty desserts. The ribbon cream pancakes were particularly good! We didn't need reservations as the Café wasn't too busy.

The menu features only sweet dishes, including pancakes, parfaits, cakes and scones all decorated in Hello Kitty style. Drinks such as tea, lattes, hot chocolate, and juice are available. When you purchase food or drinks, the staff will give you a collectable *Hello Kitty* coaster to take home as a souvenir.

TIP

The café/bakery is located right next to the Hello Kitty store.

Address: 2nd floor DiverCity Tokyo Plaza, 1-1-10 Koto, Tokyo.
Hours: 10 am-9 pm.
Closest Station: Tokyo Teleport Station, Daiba Station.

Pompompurin Café

This cute café is all about the adorable Sanrio character, Pompompurin. You can find the face of this cute golden retriever cartoon everywhere, from the walls to the menu. Even their yellow rice has Pompompurin's face on it! Photos are allowed in this café.

If you are a Pompompurin fan, there is merchandise available to purchase near the counter.

Yellow rice at the Pompompurin Café.

TIP

The wait time for the food was 30-40 mins so if you want mains and dessert, order them at the same time.
We looked at the menu while we waited to get in. This meant we could order as soon as we sat down, which helped to speed up the process!

Address: 3rd floor, Cute Cube building. 1-7-1 Jingumae Harajuku, Tokyo.
Hours: 11 am-9 pm.
Closest Station: Harajuku Station, Hachiko Exit.

Pokémon Café

This is a very cute café featuring food, drinks and merchandise all Pokémon styled. A Pokémon mascot greets you at the door and you are seated at tables with Pokémon figurines and plushies. English, Chinese, and Korean menus are also available, and the menu is seasonal.

You can order food such as the Pikachu plate which is a Pikachu-shaped rice omelette with hamburger pattie. Eevee Teriyaki Chicken Burger modelled after Eevee's face and served with a side of fries and soup. Drinks and desserts are also available such as Pokémon doughnuts. Each customer is given a cute Pokémon coaster to take home as a souvenir. There is also a Pikachu show while you eat, which is great fun, and younger children can sit down on the floor at the front and interact with him afterwards.

Pikachu at Pokémon Café.

TIPS

Bookings need to be made in advance either at the restaurant or online. Bookings can be made up to one month in advance and fill up quickly. The website is in Japanese; however, reservations can be made in English (click on the reservations tab on the right corner).

The Pokémon Centre (merchandise store) is on the same floor.

https://www.pokemoncenter-online.com/cafe/

Address: 5th floor, Nihonbashi Takashimaya East Building, 2-11-2 Nihonbashi, Chuo, Tokyo.

Hours: 10.30 am-10 pm.

Closest Station: Tokyo Station, Yaesu North Exit.

Peanuts Snoopy Cafe

This small café is dedicated to Snoopy and the other Peanuts Characters. Mainly Italian and American food such as pasta and corn dogs are served in a Snoopy theme. There are also Snoopy and Peanuts merchandise for sale and on the second-floor, vintage Snoopy items are on display. Seatings are for 90-minute time slots only.

Very cute drinks at the Peanuts Café.

TIP The café is only small and gets very busy, so make a reservation before you go to ensure a table. Reservations can be made online.

Address: 2-16-7 Aobadai, Meguro, Tokyo.,

Hours: 10 am-10 pm.

Telephone: +81 3-6452-5882.

Closest Station: Naka-Meguro Station. East Exit 2.

Owl Cafés

While not exactly a "café" I have listed this type of establishment here because of its theme like nature.

There are numerous owl cafes in Tokyo, and we visited two different ones: The Owl café village in Harajuku and Owl Cafe Akiba Fukurou in Akihabara.

Owl cafe Akiba Fukurou in Akihabara

This was the first owl café we went to and weren't sure what to expect, however, we found the owls very well looked after and the staff very attentive. Before you enter the owl area, you are given instructions on how to interact with the owls and rules to follow for the owl's comfort. For example, photography is allowed; however, flash photography and selfie sticks are not.
The staff will also take a photograph of you with the owls and present it to you at the end of your visit to take home.

Owls Squirrel, Zebra, and Gorilla having a rest.

TIPS

Bookings are only made by reservation, which can be done easily through their booking website. **http://akiba2960.com/family**

Make sure you arrive on time (or slightly earlier) for your booked time.

Children under 7 are not allowed.

The Owl café can be a little difficult to find as it is not obvious. Look for a white building next to an animal hospital. There are instructions on how to get there here.

http://akiba2960.com/access

Address: 1st Floor Akiba Fukurou Building. 67 Kanda Neribeicho, Chiyoda, Tokyo.,
Hours: Monday- Tuesday. Thursday-Friday 12-6 pm. Saturday and Sundays, 12-17 pm. Closed on Wednesdays.
Closest Station: A 3-minute walk from Akihabara Station.
Admission: 2000-yen per person, including a laminated photograph.

The Owl café village in Harajuku

This was a small, clean centre with various types of owls and a few other animals. The owls were either untethered or tethered, depending on the schedule. Photographs are allowed without a flash or selfie stick so as not to bother the birds.

We booked the 30 mins with owl and drink set. This included a souvenir, drink and 30- minutes of physical interaction with the owls (approx. 1 hour altogether). The drink area was small and cosy and allowed you to view the owls through the glass while they are resting. Once you have finished your drinks, the staff feed the owls and explain how to stroke and handle the birds before you are allowed to access the owls.
For an additional fee, you can hold the other animals in the café if you wish.

TIPS

If you want to go at a particular time you will need to make a booking as the owls are rested for an hour between sessions.

Sessions are for an hour, however, be aware that you should keep an eye on the time yourself. If you go over your allotted hour, you will be charged for extra time.

https://favy-jp.com/shops/253265

Address: ATM building, fourth floor. 1-21-15 Jingumae Harajuku, Jingumae, Shibuya, Tokyo.
Hours: 11 am-8 pm.
Closest Station: Shibuya Station, Hachiko Exit.
Admission: 800 to 2000-yen.

Cat (Neko) Cafés

Cat cafes are a type of coffee shop where customers can play with cats that roam freely around the establishment. They have become very popular, particularly in the cities where pet ownership is difficult due to small living quarters, strict rental agreements, and busy lifestyles.

Note that most places restrict entry to visitors above the age of 13.
In the Cat café, you will be charged for the amount of time you spend there, usually in 10-minute increments. You can order drinks for yourself and treats for the cats if you wish to feed them (no outside food is allowed). There are also cat toys around for you to use to play with the cats. They will ask you to sanitise your hands before entering the cat area and to remove your shoes. You can play and pat the cats; however, they don't like you to pick them up. If you are sitting on the floor and a cat climbs onto your lap, that is ok. Photography is allowed without a flash as it may disturb the cats.

There are quite a few cat cafes around Tokyo, and we visited the Temerai No Ouchi cat café in Musashino on our way to the Studio Ghibli Museum. We have a cat called Abby at home and always miss her when we go on holiday, so patting and playing with the cats was a lot of fun for us.

Temerai No Ouchi cat café

You enter the cat café through cute cat doors that open out into a large room decorated with tree-shaped beds, paw prints and a little house in the middle. The walls are painted to look as though you are in a forest and calm music was playing in the background. There are about 12 cats in all and an information book with baby pictures, descriptions, and the names of each cat so you know who they all are and their ages. You are allowed to pat the cats (no picking up) and take as many photographs as you like without a flash.

Like all cat cafes, you will be asked to wash your hands and remove your shoes before entering.

The admission price is only an entrance fee and does not include drinks or food; however, these are available to purchase at an extra fee. There are savoury dishes, desserts, hot and cold drinks available as well as beer and cocktails.

If you would like to feed the cats, you can purchase a small bowl of treats for 320-yen.

TIPS

There is free WIFI in the cafe.

Go earlier in the day on a weekday for fewer people as the café is very popular. If you want to go at the weekend, definitely make a reservation first.

The cost is less if you go on a weekday or after 7 pm.

The cat café is not far from the Studio Ghibli Museum so both can be seen in one day.

Address: 3rd floor. 2-13-14 Kichijoji Honcho, Musashino, Tokyo.
Hours: Weekdays 11 am-9 pm. Saturday and Sunday 10 am-9 pm.
Closest Station: 5-minute walk from Kichijoji Station, Central Exit.
Admission: 1200-yen for 1 hour on weekdays. 1600-yen for one hour on weekends. 700-yen after 7 pm.

Entrance to the Temerai No Ouchi cat café

Mogu Mogu Hamster Café

This cute "café" is run by the same owners as Harry the Hedgehog Café, only this one has hamsters. The café is located just off the main shopping street of Roppongi and makes a nice break from retail shopping and sightseeing. While not really a café as they don't serve food or drink, it's still a fun place to visit with kids.

You can pat the hamsters and purchase "Hamster Snacks" to feed them if you wish.

Hamster at the Mogu Mogu Café

TIPS

Like all these animal style cafes keep an eye on your time (which can be difficult when you are having fun with the animals!) If you go over your 30-minute time slot even by a minute you will be charged for an extra half an hour! You can stay longer than 30 mins, just be aware you will be charged in 30 min time slots.

There are rules at the café which the staff will inform you about before you can play with the hamsters, such as sanitising your hands before touching the animals, sitting while petting the hamsters and being gentle with them. These are for the Hamster's safety.

There is a drink vending machine at the café, or you can bring your own food and drink, just don't feed it to the hamsters!

Weekdays are less busy at the café.

http://www.harinezumi-cafe.com/en/
Address: 6-7-2, Iwahori Building, third floor, Roppongi, Minato City, Tokyo.
Hours: 11 am -7 pm.
Nearest Station: A one-minute walk from Roppongi Station. Also, Roppongi Itchome Metro Station.
Admission: 30 minutes is 1300-yen per person. Hamster snacks 1500-yen.

Harry Hedgehog Café

There are several Harry Hedgehog Cafes in Tokyo, all have Hedgehogs, and some have other animals as well, such as Otters. We visited the one in Harajuku.
You will be given gloves to handle the Hedgehogs during your visit. The "café" only has self-serve drinks available. However, you can bring your own food.

TIPS

There are rules at the café which the staff will inform you about before you can play with the Hedgehogs, such as sanitising your hands before touching the animals, sitting while petting the hedgehogs and being gentle with them. Children under 12 need to be supervised. These rules are for the animal's safety.

Reservations can be made online or just turn up at the store and try your luck! Weekdays are less busy.

Keep an eye on your time. If you go over your 30-minute time slot you will be charged for an extra half an hour! You can stay longer than 30 mins, just be aware you will be charged in 30 min time slots.

Address: 1-13-21 Jingumae. Fourth floor, Shibuya, Tokyo.
Hours: 11 am -7 pm.
Nearest Station: Harajuku Station.

Admission: 30 minutes is 1300-yen per person. Hedgehog snacks 1500-yen.

Maid Cafés

Maid cafes where the staff dress up as maids, are a popular theme restaurant idea. Some of the Maid cafes are a little sleazy. However, we found the Maidreamin Digitized Cafe and Dining Bar in Shibuya to be fun and friendly. The staff in these style restaurants act very cute and often childlike, however, if you are prepared to go along with this, it can be fun.
The Shibuya branch of Maidreamin has an interior that looks as though it is part of a video game. Cube-shaped lights that change colour hang from the ceiling, the walls are decorated with Japanese emoji and the panels in the walls are animated.

Photos of the venue are not allowed; however, you can take photos of your food if you wish. If you want a photograph with your waitress/server (taken on a mini-instant camera), the cost is 500-yen, and they will decorate it for you. There are also combo packages available for food, drink, photo etc.

The venue is smoking (no nonsmoking section available).
Free WIFI is available for customers.

TIP The cafe is located downstairs in the Horaiya Building. To find the café look for the lit-up sign with a picture of the maids by the stairs.

https://maidreamin.com/multilp/

Address: Horaiya building. Basement floor. 30-1 Udagawacho Shibuya, Tokyo.
Hours: Monday-Thursday 3 pm-11 pm. Friday 3 pm-5 pm. Saturday 3 pm-5 pm. Sunday 1 pm-11 pm.
Closest Station: Shibuya Station, Hachiko Exit.

Ninja Restaurant

Ninja Akasaka is a ninja-themed restaurant based on an Edo era village. This isn't just a novelty restaurant; the food was amazing and delicious - good choices of courses including vegetarian, vegan and a children's menu. You get your own booth with sliding doors, which is great for groups and families. The ninja magic at your table was great fun too.

To get to your table, you must venture down a dark passageway, which may be frightening for smaller children. As most themed restaurants, the price for the food is not cheap, however, you are paying for the "experience" and entertainment.

Reservations can be made online, or by telephone. Bookings are for a 2-hour time slot, and you must be on time for your booking.

https://ninjaakasaka.com/en/experience/

Address: 1st floor Akasaka Tokyu Plaza. 2-14-3 Nagatacho, Chiyoda, Tokyo.

Telephone: +81 3-5157-3936.

Hours: 7 pm-10 pm.

Closest Station: 3 minutes' walk from Akasakamitsuke Station. Ginza line 3.

Animate Café Ikebukuro

This Anime café is located inside the 7 floor Animate building on the 7th and 8th floors and has a complicated procedure to visit. 1st you have to make a reservation which can be done at the café or online in advance. However, this does not guarantee you a table. Once you arrive at the café on your day of choice, you are then placed into a lottery to see what time you can enter the café. The café has different anime themes depending on the month, and this will determine the drinks and food available at that time as they will be related to the particular theme. When you purchase food or a drink, you will also be given a collectable souvenir coaster of that anime.
Advanced reservations can be made from the website below; however, the website is in Japanese so you will need to use Google translate or similar to translate first.

https://cafe.animate.co.jp/shop/ikebukuro/

Address: 7th and 8th floors Animate Building. 3-2-1 Higashiikebukuro, Toshima, Tokyo.
Hours: 7th floor 11: 30-8 pm. 8th floor 12: 30- 9 pm.
Closest Station: 8-minute walk from Ikebukuro Station.

Drinks at the Animate Café

There is also a second Animate café (Animate Ikebukuro2), located in Ikebukuro and will have a different Anime theme from the others. The second cafe has the same reservation and lottery system as the first and is located on the fourth floor of the second Animate store.

https://cafe.animate.co.jp/shop/ikebukuro_2/

Address: 4th floor Animate Building, 1-21-13 Higashi Ikebukuro Tokyo.
Hours: 11 am-9.30 pm.
Closest Station: 6-minute walk from Ikebukuro Station.

Goodsmile/Animate Café Akihabara

This Anime café is a collaboration between Animate and Goodsmile and again has different anime themes depending on which anime they are displaying at the time. The café is located on the 5th floor of the figurine shop RASHIBAN.
Like the other Animate cafes, you will most likely need to make a reservation and they also have the lottery system for the time slot you will be given for seating.

Drinks at the Goodsmile/Animate Café

TIPs

As this is a smaller café than the main one in Ikebukuro, if you go during the week, you may be able to get in without a reservation if it is not too busy.

Make a reservation online, go to the café when it opens and receive a ticket (by lottery) for your allocated time, go and do some other shopping or sightseeing, then return for your allocated time slot. Don't be late or your table will be re-allocated!
https://cafe.animate.co.jp/shop/akihabara/

Address: 5th floor of Rashiban figure shop. 1-7-6 Sotokanda, Akihabara, Tokyo.
Hours: 11 am-9.30 pm.
Closest Station: 5-minute walk from Akihabara Station. Or Suehirocho Subway, Tokyo Metro Ginza Line.

ARTNIA Square Enix Cafe

This interesting café, which is shaped like a giant white egg, is themed after the video game company, Square Enix the developers of Final Fantasy, Black Butler, Dragon Quest and the Kingdom Hearts Anime Series. There is a Final Fantasy display area including a crystal waterfall, surrounded by elaborately crafted figurines and artworks with Final Fantasy tunes playing in the background.

The café has food, drinks and merchandise all based on Final Fantasy, Kingdom Hearts, and their other anime series, such as key chains, plushies and mobile phone covers.

Strawberry Pancakes at Artnia Square Enix Cafe

http://www.jp.square-enix.com/artnia/

Address: First floor Shinjuku East Side Square, 6-27-30 Shinjuku, Tokyo.
Hours: 11 am-10 pm.
Closest Station: Shinjuku Station, East Exit

Final Fantasy Café Eorzea

The Final Fantasy Café in Akihabara is based off the Final Fantasy series with this particular café modelled off the Carline Canopy building in Final Fantasy XIV. The café is decorated with weapons, and artifacts and the food and drinks are inspired by the show. For example, you can order, Bahamut Gigaflare Indian curry, Ahriman Monburan (chestnut) cake, Cactuar Matcha (green tea) ice cream, and Moogle honey toast. The drinks include black magic blackcurrant tea, Cactuar juice, Good King Moggle Mog XII's tropical pineapple juice, and plenty of potions. A collectable Final Fantasy Café is provided with your drinks order.
There is also an area in the cafe where customers can play Final Fantasy XIV: A Realm Reborn.

At the moment the café has a lottery-style entry system where you line up at 10.00 am (You can get there at 9.30 am and start to queue if you're keen). At 10.30 am the staff ask one member of your group to choose a number from a bag which will determine your allotted time slot. As there are only limited seats in the cafe, if you choose a number greater than 50 you will not be given a seat and will have to come back on another day.

The time slots available are:
11:30 to 13:30
14:00 to 16:00
16:30 to 18:30
19:00 to 22:00
As you can see, time slots 1 through 3 are 120 minutes and time slot 4 is 180 minutes.
This café is a smoking venue and does not have a non-smoking section.

TIPS The café gets super busy on the weekends, so try to go on a weekday.
Tickets can be bought a few days in advance from a Lawsons convenience store.

The lottery allocation closes at 10.45 so get there earlier than 10 am.
When you are in the cafe, you order using an order sheet and can order as many things as you like within your time slot. Billing is based on the order sheets, so if you want to pay together, use the same order sheet.

Free Wi-Fi is available.

Address: Pasela Resort Akihabara. 1-1-10 SotoKanda, 2nd Floor, Chiyoda-Ku, Tokyo.

Hours: 11.30-10 pm in two hour allocated timeslots, (see above).

Closest Station: Akihabara Station, Electric Town Exit.

2D Café

This new café is a unique and amazing looking venue. Everything inside the café is designed to look like it is a 2D drawing straight out of a cartoon or comic!
Photographs are allowed and you can take some cool-looking photos.
The food menu consists of mainly drinks and desserts such as fruit bowls and parfaits, so more of a stop for morning or afternoon tea rather than lunch or dinner.

Address: 1-7-5 Hyakunin-cho Shinjuku, Tokyo.
Hours: 11 am-11 pm.
Nearest Station: Okubo Station.

Inside the 2D café.

Pepper Parlor Café -Robot Café

If you love robots and electronics, you should take a visit to the Pepper Parlor Café. It is something you can't really experience outside of Japan. When you first enter the café, it seems as though you are entering a sci fi movie as there are robots or Pepper-Kun everywhere. The Pepper-Kun, or robots, are used to place your order and to pay for your food. Your food is then served by *real* people!

There are drinks available to purchase and food such as waffles which you customize to your liking. Merchandise is also for sale at the café.

Address: 1-2-3 Dogenzaka Shibuya, Tokyo.

Hours: 11am-9 pm.

Nearest Station: Yamamoto line, Shibuya Station.

Pepper-Kun inside the Pepper Parlor Café.

Godaime Hanayama Udon Café

If you are a fan of Tanaki and udon, then you will want to visit the Godaime Hanayama Udon café. Located in Ginza this very popular udon café serves itrs dishes in cute tanaki style bowls and plates. The café specialises in Himokawa Udon (extra wide softer noodles), however other dishes such as tempura and curry sets can be ordered.

The queues to get into this restaurant can be long so you may also want to try their other café in Nihonbashi.

Tanaki Udon

Address: Floor one Welfare Building 3 Chome-14-13 Ginza, Tokyo

Hours: 11am-4 pm. 6-10pm

Nearest Station: 2-minute walk from Higashi Ginza station

Chapter Nine

Top Shopping Spots

Animated characters are very popular, and there are a number of shops around Tokyo and Osaka where you can purchase all types of merchandise from plush toys to stationery and mobile phone covers. There are also many "Gashapon" machines where you deposit a coin into the machine, twist a lever and a little collectable toy drops out.

There are also quite a few adult stores in this area of Japan.

Gaming, figurines, collectables and comics

Akihabara.

The main shopping strip in Akihabara is on Chuo Dori and the blocks that surround it.

Popular Stores include:

Mandarake
K-books,
Kinokuniya
Book off
Animate
Akihabara Gamers Main Store
Super Potato
Comic Toranoana
Kotobukiya
Asobit
Kaiyodo
Volks
Radio Kaikan
Sega Mega store
Laox
Lashinban

Mandarake Akihabara

The ground floor has a "Japanese Pop Antique" section of rare, vintage figures—many are worth hundreds of thousands of yen. Also on the first floor are the counters for selling your unwanted goods. The second-floor houses dolls, "magical girls toys" (Sailor

Moon etc.) and cosplay items. Continuing up, the third floor has regular manga that you might be familiar with.

The fourth and fifth floors are stocked with *doujinshi* (independently published comics), and adult comics. The fourth floor is geared towards men, while the fifth-floor stocks genres typically popular with women—such as Boys Love Manga.

The sixth-floor stocks DVDs, Blu-Ray and game software The seventh and eighth floors stock a variety of toys and collectibles, including robots, anime figures, trading cards, stickers, as well as model cars and trains.

Figurines for sale in Akihabara

Ikebukuro

The Evangelion Store

Located in Ikebukuro, the Evangelion Store is a wonderful place to shop for fans of the series. The store is quite small, however, sells a range of Evangelion products including clothing, stationery, art books and other merchandise. There is also a statue of Rei and figurines from the Evangelion series in the store.

Statue of Rei from the Evangelion series

TIPS There are two Parco shopping malls in Ikebukuro so make sure you go to the P'Parco one for the Evangelion store. Sunshine City is nearby where you will also find Namja Town and Pokémon Mega Tokyo.
https://www.evastore2.jp/tokyo-01/

Address: 2nd floor P'Parco shopping mall in Ikebukuro. 1-50-3-5 Higashiikebukuro, Tokyo.
Hours: 11-9 pm.
Closest Station: JR Ikebukuro Station, East Exit.

Otome road

Otome Road or Maiden Road is a popular shopping spot or female fans of Japanese anime and manga. Otome Road is a great place to purchase Doujinshi (Japanese Indie Manga). You will also find Anime and manga merchandise specializing in content targeted to the female audience, as well as Yaoi/Boy love manga. Be aware, if any Doujinshi is sealed in plastic, it usually means it contains adult content.

Nearest Station: 9-minute walk from lkebukuro Station, East Exit, JR Line. Or 6-minute walk from Higashi-lkebukuro Station, Subway Yurakucho Line.

Display inside Animate/Goodsmile Cafe

Some of the stores along Otome Road include:

Animate Flagship Store

There are two Animate branches in Ikebukuro: a small one where special pop-up cafe events are held and the main store, which is seven stories tall. Merchandise such as original CDs, DVDs, manga, novels, keychains, accessories, fans, mugs, bookmarks, shirts, smartphone cases and just about everything else anime and j-pop related can be found here. The animate cafe and the animate cafe shop can also be found in this building. The cafe hosts themed events and reservations are usually required for these.

Address: 3-2-1 Higashi Ikebukuro, Tokyo.
Hours: 11.30-9.30 pm.

Mandarake selling used and new goods, including comics and anime-related merchandise. Note this store is not suitable for younger children as some products feature nudity/skimpy outfits. Parents' discretion is advised.

Address: 3 Higashiikebukuro, Toshima-Ku, Tokyo.
Hours: 12-8.30 pm Daily.

K-Books

K-Books sells manga and books plus other merchandise such as pins, dolls, games, and cosplay items such as wigs, costumes, and props.
There are three K-Book stores on Otome Road each specialising in different products.

www.k-books.co.jp/news/2015/test/k-books-en/_index.html#ikebukuro

K-Books Dougin-kan

Address: Syouwa Building 3-12-12, Higashiikebukuro, Toshima-Ku, Tokyo.
2nd floor sells fan-made comics (Doujinshi) and female related fan merchandise such as Yaoi/Boylove manga.
The 3rd floor sells secondhand merchandise and collectors' items.
Hours: 11:00-8 pm.

K-Books Cosplay

Selling cosplay costumes, wigs, and related merchandise for women. Also includes second-hand costumes.

Address: Higashiikebukuro Building, first floor. 3-11-1, Higashiikebukuro, Toshima-Ku, Tokyo.

Hours: 11-8 pm daily.

K-Books Comic-Kan

Selling manga, posters, Boylove fan art.

Address: Higashiikebukuro, first floor. 3-15-14, Higashiikebukuro, Toshima-Ku Tokyo.

Hours: 11:00-8 pm.

Ginza Hakuhinkan Toy Park

Address: 8-8-11 Ginza, Chuo-Ku, Tokyo.
Hours: 11:00-8 pm.
Closest Station: Ginza, Shimbashi.

TIP Many of the theme cafes in Tokyo also sell figurines and merchandise related to their café, such as the Final Fantasy Cafes and Animate cafes.

See the section on theme cafes for more information on these eateries.

Pokémon

For fans of the popular television series there are several Pokémon stores around Tokyo including:

Pokemon Tokyo Bay located within La La Port Tokyo Bay open 10-8pm

Pokemon Sky Tree located within the Tokyo Solamachi retail complex open 10-9pm

Pokemon Tokyo Station located in the Character Street shopping area inside Tokyo Station
Open 10-8.30pm

Pokemon Mega Town is the largest Pokemon store located within the Sunshine City shopping complex in Ikebukuro. Open 10-8pm

Trading cards, collectable figures, plushies and capsule toys can all be purchased in these stores.

Cosplay costumes

Gee Store

Address: 3-15-5, Sotokanda, Chiyoda-Ku, Tokyo.
Hours: 11-8 pm. 11-7 pm Sunday.
Nearest Station: 10-minute walk from Akihabara Station, JR Line. Or 3-minute walk from Suehirocho Station, Tokyo Metro Ginza Line.

Mandarake Nakano Broadway

Address: Nakano Broadway shopping Centre. 5-52-15 Nakano, Nakano City.
Hours: 12-8 pm daily.
Nearest Station: 5-minute walk from JR Nakano Station, North Exit.

Nakano Broadway branch of Mandarake

K-Books

There are several branches of this store throughout Tokyo. They sell wigs, costumes, accessories, and all cosplay gear.

One store is in Ikebukuro.
Address: 3-12-5 Higashi Ikebukuro Toshima Ku Tokyo.
Hours: 11.30-8 pm Mon-Fri. 11-8 pm Sat and Sun.
Nearest Station: 9-minute walk from JR Ikebukuro Station, East Exit. Or a 6-minute walk from Higashi-Ikebukuro Station, Metro Yurakucho Line.

Japanese sweets

Japanese sweets

Japanese sweets are small and brightly coloured, often featuring the images of characters such as Hello Kitty, Neko Cat, or anime characters.

They can be found in markets and smaller shops such as Tokyu Hands and Dasio and make inexpensive presents for the kids to take home for their friends.

Flavoured KitKats

Apple flavoured Kit Kat chocolate

Whenever we take a trip to Japan, we love to bring home a few packets of KitKats!
They have such unusual flavours and make interesting gifts to take home. Some of the flavours we have tried are red apple, sakura (cherry blossom), Matcha (green tea), strawberry cheesecake, sweet potato, raspberry dark chocolate, passionfruit, café au late and crème brulee. There are also some crazier ones like soy sauce, hot chilli, vegetable juice, wasabi, miso soup, green bean, and cough drop.

TIPS

The flavours available are rotated by the company, so not all of them are available at the same time. Special gift-wrapped ones are available from the KitKat chocolatiers store. However, you can buy them at a lower price from convenience stores like Lawsons and Family Mart.

Another great place to purchase bags of KitKats is from Don Quijote stores which often have a large range at a lower price.

Vending Machines

Vending machines are located everywhere, particularly train stations, entrances to parks and attractions and along streets. You can purchase all kinds of items from the vending machines.

TIP The vending machines usually require yen or sometimes IC cards such as the Pasmo or Suica can be used to purchase items. Foreign credit cards are not accepted.

Hot chocolate in a bottle from a vending machine

Some of the interesting items we have seen for sale in vending machines are:

Hot and cold drinks in the same machine.

Frozen slushies (the drink comes out as regular liquid coke, however, when you turn it upside down, it turns into a slushie!)

Clean t-shirts and underwear.
Individually wrapped neckties.

Umbrellas

Fresh flowers in a gift basket.

Fresh individual apples and bananas

Hot soup and other meals in a can.

Hot chocolate in a can or bottle (lovely on a cold day).

Vending machine featuring characters from Hyouka

Toys, plushies and other collectibles

Kiddyland

A huge toy store full of all kinds of toys from plushies, to collectables, stationery, and clothing. Brace yourself, this place gets extremely busy!

Address: 6-1-9 Omotesando Harajuku, Tokyo.
Hours: 11-9 pm Mon-Fri. 10.30-9 pm Sat and Sun.
Nearest Station: Harajuku Station.

Plushies for sale in Kiddyland

Snoopy town

This store is located in Tokyo Station "Character Street" and sells all kinds of Snoopy products from plushy toys to stationery and snacks.

Address: Basement Level 1, Character Street, Tokyo Station, Tokyo.
Hours: 10 am-8.30 pm.

One-Piece

One-Piece Store - Mugiwara

Firstly, there are two One-Piece Stores.
The first is located on level one, of Foot Town in Tokyo Tower and is called Mugiwara Store. This character store located in Tokyo Tower along with a One-Piece café and restaurant, plus the One-Piece Amusement centre is a fan paradise. We saw lots of merchandise all relating to One-Piece characters here from t-shirts and caps to Stationery, character food and collectables.

Entrance to the One-Piece Store - Mugiwara

Address: Level one, Foot Town, Tokyo Tower. 4-2-8 Shiba Park, Minato-Ku Tokyo.
Hours: 10 am-10.00 pm daily.
Nearest Station: 5-minute walk from Akabanebashi Station, Toei Oedo line.
6-minute walk from Kamiyacho Station, Exit 1. Or 15-minute walk from JR Yamanote Line Station, North Exit.
Admission: Free.

One-Piece Store - Tongari Island

The second store is located within the One-Piece Tower and can only be accessed when you pay to go into the theme park. Again, it has loads of One-Piece character items and collectables for sale such as key rings, file covers, charms and limited-edition items.

Address: Level three, Foot Town, Tokyo Tower. 4-2-8 Shiba Park, Minato-Ku Tokyo.
Hours: 10 am-10.00 pm daily.
Nearest Station: 5-minute walk from Akabanebashi Station, Toei Oedo line.
6-minute walk from Kamiyacho Station, Exit 1.
15-minute walk from JR Yamanote Line Station, North Exit.
Admission: entry included in One-Piece Tower theme park.

One Piece merchandise for sale

Hello Kitty Konguriyaki

Get ready for cuteness overload when you visit the Hello Kitty store in Odaiba, located on the 2nd floor of the Diver City mall. In this store, you will find Hello Kitty, Kero Keroppi, Gudetama, My Melody and Pochacco. There is a large Gudetama corner, plus a huge collection of plushies, t-shirts, collectibles, and other souvenirs. Also, Hello Kitty Gashapon (capsule machines) with collectable Hello Kitty pins.

Hello Kitty merchandise

TIP There is a Hello Kitty café/bakery right next door which serves ice cream, pancakes, and other baked goods all Hello Kitty and friends themed.

Address: 2nd floor DiverCity, Tokyo Plaza, 1-1-10 Koto, Tokyo.
Hours: 10 am-9 pm.
Closest Station: Tokyo Teleport Station, Daiba Station.

Fashion

Shibuya 109

A very popular spot for shopping, there are about 120 shops over 10 floors in Shibuya 109. My daughters loved shopping here as it is full of Japanese fashion, accessories, and beauty product stores. Since it opened in 1979, the mall has grown to gain almost a cult following as the epicentre of Tokyo's "gyaru" subculture.

Shibuya 109 Fashion Store

https://www.shibuya109.jp/
Address: 2-29-1 Dogenzaka, Shibuya City, Tokyo.
Hours: 10 am-9 pm.
Closest Station: Shibuya Station, JR Line, Hachiko Exit.
TIPS The statue of the famous Japanese dog Hachiko stands across the road from the 109 complex at the entrance/exit to the Shibuya Station.
There is also a *Shibuya 109 Men's* Store across the road with men's/boy's fashion.

Ragtag

Ragtag is a clothing store located in branches across Japan, specialising in second-hand designer clothing for men and women. The main store is located on Cat Street Harajuku spans three floors. The ground floor is reserved for fancier designers such as Vivienne Westwood, Diesel, Marc Jacobs, and Chanel. The second-floor houses casual and streetwear such as A Bathing Ape, Hysteric Glamour and Journal Standard. The third floor has designer handbags where you can take a peek at Chanel, Louis Vuitton, and Hermès fashion.

Address: 6-14-2 Cat Street Jingumae, Shibuya, Tokyo.
Hours: 11 am-8 pm.

nearest Station: Harajuku Station, Yamanote line, Omotesando Exit. Meiji-Jingumae Station, Chiyoda and Fukutoshin lines. Omotesando Station, Ginza, Hanzomon and Chiyoda lines, Exit A1.

Dog

Dog is a basement boutique store selling vintage clothing and original outfits. www.dog-hjk.com

Address: Basement floor, 3-23-3 Jingumae, Shibuya, Tokyo.
Hours: 12-8 pm.
Nearest Station: Harajuku Station, Yamanote line. Meiji-Jingumae Station, Chiyoda and Fukutoshin lines.

Liz Lisa

Liz Lisa is a popular fashion for young women. The clothes, bags, shoes, hats etc are all very frilly and cute. All the items have little touches like bows, ribbons, and lace. There are several stores throughout the country, and Tokyo has two. The main one is located in the Shibuya 109 building in Shibuya. Level 6.

Fashion from Liz Lisa

Address: Shibuya 109 Store, 6th floor. 2-29-1 Dogenzaka, Shibuya City, Tokyo.
Hours: 10 am-9 pm.
Nearest Station: Shibuya Station, JR Yammamoto line, Hachiko Exit.

Laforet

Laforet is a fashionable shopping mall with numerous popular stores. There is also a very busy food mall.

https://www.laforet.ne.jp/en/

Address: 1-11-6 Jingumae, Shibuya City, Tokyo.
Hours: 11-9 pm.
Nearest Station: Meiji-jingumae Station, Chiyoda Line, Exit 5.

Wego

This is one of the most popular street fashion retailers for teens in Tokyo. Wego is well-known as one of the trendiest places to pick up casual clothing at a reasonable price.
The main store is located on Meiji Street in Shibuya Tokyo. There is also a store in the Shibuya 109 department store.

https://wegoec.jp/shop/

Address: 6-5-3 Jingumae, Shibuya, Tokyo.
Hours: 10 am-8.30 pm.
Nearest Station: Harajuku Station.

Bodyline and Boutique Takenoko

These stores have a little bit of everything for people seeking out the trendiest of looks. Bodyline offers everyday clothing, also Lolita-style dresses, and cosplay clothing.

.

Address: 1-6-15 Jingumae, Shibuya, Tokyo.
Hours: 11 am-8 pm.
Nearest Station: Harajuku Station. Meiji Jingue Mae Station.

UNIQLO Flagship Store

If you're looking for everyday Japanese brand clothes, this store is a cheaper alternative to high-end fashion. They have a children's section too. There are several Uniqlo stores throughout Tokyo and other parts of Japan, however, the one in Ginza is one of the largest.

TIP check the glassed-in walkway to the nearby building for a steep look down!

Address: 6-9-5 Ginza, Chuo-Ku, Tokyo.
Hours: 11:00-9 pm daily.
Closest Station: Ginza Station.

H and M

This well-known clothing store selling men's, women's and children's clothing has branches all over Japan. The store in Shibuya is the largest and very popular.

Address: 1-8-10 Jingumae Shibuya, Tokyo.
Hours: Mon-Thu 10:00 am- 9:00 pm. Fri 10:00 am-10:00 pm. Sat 9:30 am-10:00 pm. Sun 9:30 am-9:00 pm.
Nearest Station: Harajuku Station. Or Meji-Jingumae Station.

Forever 21

This popular clothing fashion store has several outlets throughout the country. One of the largest is in Shinjuku.

www.forever21.co.jp

Address: 3-1-13 Shinjuku, Shinjuku, Tokyo.
Nearest Station: Kiyosumi Sharakawa Station.

Stationery

The Japanese love stationery, pens, file covers, stickers, note pads, everything cute and colourful. Stationery can be found in specialist stores throughout Tokyo. For a less expensive variety look in these chain stores:

Daiso

This 100-yen ($1) shop is a very popular store selling all kinds of products including stationery such as stickers, pens, food shaped erasers, decorated paper, and file dividers. There are over 3000 stores located throughout Japan, including several in Tokyo. Daiso stores can be small or larger sized depending on where they are located. For a better range of products and experience, visit one of the larger Daiso shops.

Erasers from Daiso

There is a large Daiso Store in the Decks shopping mall in Daiba Tokyo.

Address: Decks Mall, Tokyo Beach, 1-6-1 Daiba, Minato-Ku.
Hours: 11 am-9 pm.

Tokyu-Hands.

This discount chain store selling all manner of goods is situated all throughout Japan. Look for the green and white sign.

There is a large Tokyu-Hands store in Shinjuku.

Address: Times Square Building. 2nd to 8th floors. 5-24-2 Sendagaya, Shibuya-ku Tokyo.

And also, in Ikebukuro.

Address: 1-28-10 Higashi-Ikebukuro, Toshima-ku, Tokyo.

Don Quijote

Don Quijote is another store that sells all kinds of items for a low-price including stationery. They have several stores, including one in Ikebukuro, Akihabara, and Shinjuku.

Don Quijote Shinjuku Branch

Shinjuku Kabukicko Branch

Address: 1-16-5 Kabukicho, Shinjuku, Tokyo.
Hours: open 24 hours!
Nearest Station: Shinjuku Station, East Exit.

Markets

The markets in Japan are a great place to try freshly made Japanese snacks, such as *osenbei* (rice crackers), *ningyo-yaki* (a sweet cake filled with sweet red bean paste pressed into the shape of a doll or character such as Hello Kitty) or *Dango* (round balls of *mochi or* sticky rice topped with various flavourings such as sweet soy glaze). Cute colourful Japanese sweets, hand fans and other trinkets can be purchased at the markets and make great gifts to take home for friends.
Some markets we visited on our holidays were:

Nakamise shopping street in Asakusa with its' colourful stalls. The start of the main shopping street is just past the huge red lantern Kaminarimon gate of Senso-Ji Temple, right near the Asakusa Station exit. Note that the shops in the market close relatively early. Great place to buy sweets, cakes, and other souvenirs.

Sweets for sale at Nakamise markets

Address: Asakusa, Taitō-Ku, Tokyo.
Hours: each store is different.
Nearest Station: Asakusa Station.
Admission: Free.

Ameyoko Market Street. This outdoor market is famous for its traditional style stores selling spices, seafood, vegetables, and all sorts of bargains. There are over 400 stores lining this busy market street that sits under the JR Ueno railway line. You can hear the train as it whisks overhead. If you want to see where the locals shop this lively and interesting market is the place to go.

Masks for sale at Ameyoko Markets

TIPS

Ueno Park and Ueno Zoo are close by to this market. Buy some lunch or snacks to take with you before you head to the park or zoo.

A website of the markets can be accessed here: however, it is in Japanese, so you will need Google Translate or a similar app to translate the page into English.

http://www.ameyoko.net/

Address: Ueno, Taito. Tokyo.
Nearest Station: 5-minute walk from Ueno Station, central Exit. JR Okachimachi Station, North Exit.
Admission: Free.

Music

Big Love music store.

Big Love Music is an independent record store that collects vinyl and cassette tapes of indie bands from the US, the UK and Europe.

www.bigloverecords.jp

Address: 3rd floor Houei Building. 2-31-3 Jingumae, Shibuya. Tokyo.
Hours: 1 pm-10 pm Tuesday-Sunday. 3 pm-8 pm Mondays.
Nearest Station: Harajuku Station, Yamamoto line.

Electronics

We found the best place to buy electronics, camera equipment etc. was from Yodobashi Camera, Bic Camera or Laox stores. These can be found all over Tokyo, particularly in Akihabara, Shibuya, Shinjuku, and Ikebukuro. Be aware of voltage differences when buying electronics and regional differences if purchasing DVD's or games as they may not play in your home country.

Yodobashi Camera

Akihabara Store

The branch of Yodobashi Camera in Akihabara is a huge building full of computers, cameras, and electronics.

TIPS There are toilets facilities available in this store, tax-free shopping and free Wi-Fi. Remember to bring your passport if you want to shop duty-free.

Address: 1-1 Kanda Hanaokacho, Chiyoda, Akihabara. Tokyo.
Hours: 9.30 am-10.30 pm daily.
Nearest Station: Akihabara Station. Denkigai Exit.

Shinjuku West Main store

Another large Yodobashi Camera store is located in Shinjuku.

TIPS There are toilets facilities in this store.

Address: 1-11-1 Nishishinjuku, Shinjuku, Tokyo.
Hours: 9.30 am-10 pm daily.
Nearest Station: Shinjuku Station, JR Yamamoto line, West Exit.

Bic Camera

Ikebukuro Store

8 floors selling everything from mobile phones and games to iPads and beauty products.

TIPS There is also free Wi-Fi, airport delivery of your purchases and tax-free shopping available so remember to bring your passport if you want to shop duty free.

Address: 1-41-5, Higashiikebukuro, Toshima-Ku, Tokyo.
Hours: 10 am-10 pm daily.
Nearest Station: Ikebukuro Station, East Exit.

Akihabara Store

7 floors with electronic toys, camera equipment, computers, and electrical appliances.

Address: 4-1-1, Sotokanda, Chiyoda-Ku, Tokyo.
Hours: 10 am-9 pm daily.
Nearest Station: Akihabara Station, Denkigai Exit.

Laox

Laox stores are a great place to shop if you are looking for Tax-Free items. Apart from electronics such as cameras and computers, they also sell watches, jewellery and cosmetics.

Akihabara Store

Address: Kinokuniya Building. 1st floor. 1-2-14 Sotokanda, Chiyoda Ku, Tokyo.
Hours: 10 am-7 pm daily.
Nearest Station: Akihabara Station, Electric Town Exit (south side).

Shinjuku Main Store

https://www.laox.co.jp/laox_store/en/shinjuku/

TIP tax-free shopping is available in these stores so bring your passport if you wish to purchase products duty free.

Address: 5th to 8th Floors, MetLife/JTB, Shinjuku Square Building. 3-1-20 Shinjuku. Tokyo.
Hours: 9 am-9 pm daily.
Nearest Station: Shinjuku Station.

Other souvenirs

Oriental Bazaar

This is a great store to purchase pottery, kimonos, yukata, sake sets, decorated chopsticks, lacquerware and other souvenirs to take home. There are three floors, each selling different items. I bought a lovely Yukata from here on our first visit to Japan. Kiddyland is also right down the road from the Oriental Bazaar.

http://www.orientalbazaar.co.jp/en/index.html

Address: 9-13 5 Jingumae, Shibuya, Tokyo.
Hours: 10 am -7 pm. Closed on Thursdays.
Closest Station: 5-minute walk JR Yamanote Line, Harajuku Station, Omotesando Exit. Or 4-minute walk, Tokyo Metro Chiyoda Line, Omotesando Station, Exit B4.

Don Quijote

Don Quijote stores are a great place for the kids to shop for souvenirs to take home and for quirky gifts to take home for their friends without breaking the budget. You can purchase all types of items including hand fans, beauty face masks and Japanese beauty products, cute food and animal erasers, KitKats in numerous flavours, sweets and cookies and many other products.

TIPS these stores all have free WIFI.

Some of the products are tax-free for foreign visitors.

The Shinjuku and Akihabara branches of Don Quijote can deliver products purchased to the airport if you don't want to carry them around.

Akihabara's Don Quijote is a huge location with its own theatre where popular idol groups perform. It is also known for its wide variety of anime and manga related goods.

Shinjuku Kabukicko Branch

Address: 1-16-5 Kabukicho, Shinjuku, Tokyo.

Hours: open 24 hours!

Nearest Station: Shinjuku Station, East Exit.

Akihabara Branch

Address: 4-3-3 Sotokanda, Chiyoda City, Akihabara, Tokyo.

Hours: 9 am-1 am daily.

Nearest Station: 3-minute walk from JR Akihabara Station, Electric Town Exit on the JR Yamanote Line. JR Sobu Line, Tokyo Metro Hibiya Line or Tokyo Metro Ginza Line.

Don Quijote Branch Ginza

Ginza Branch

Address: 2-10 Asakusa, Taito-Ku, Tokyo.

Hours: open 24 hours!

Nearest Station: 1-minute walk from Tsukuba Express, Asakusa Station, Exit 1.

Or 5-minute walk from Ginza Line Tawaramachi Station, Exit 2.

Sweet potato KitKats from Don Quijote

Gallery Marusan (Maru dog shop and gallery)

Gallery Marusan located ten minutes by train from Shinjuku Station is dedicated to Maru the Shiba Inu dog, famous on Instagram. There are scarves, stationery, key chains, stickers, and all sorts of merchandise available featuring pictures of Maru.

TIP Ueno Zoo and Ueno Park are both nearby and worth visiting.

Address: 2-12-3 Nezu, Bunkyo City, Tokyo.
Hours: 11-6 pm. Closed on Mondays.
Closest Station: Nezu Metro Station. Ueno Station.

Adult Stores

M's

M's in Akihabara is an infamous seven-level sex shop purportedly one of the largest in the world.
The seven levels have all the things for all types and all the possible kinks and it's an interesting place to pick up a few "only in Japan" items to take home as souvenirs. Even if you're not in the market, a quick look can be quite educational! Look for the lime green sign.

Address 1 15-13 Sotokanda, Chiyoda, Tokyo 1 minute walk from the Electric Town South Exit of JR Akihabara Station.
Hours: 10am-11pm
Closest Station Akihabara Station

Department Stores

Department stores are a great place to window shop when the weather is rainy or hot. They are often large; however, so be sure to keep hold of young children's hands.

TIP The food halls in department stores are amazing and worth taking a look at for the dessert/cake sections alone! Most food halls are found in the basement levels of the department stores.

Takashimaya Department Store.

The Takashima Department Store is amazing shopping complex with lots of stores including a Kinokuniya bookstore selling Japanese and English books, Tokyu Hands and Uniqlo clothing store.
Restaurants are located on the 12-14th floors, with the *White Garden* on the thirteenth floor lit up at night and a green oasis during the day. Definitely worth a look.

The basement B1 is where you'll find the amazing food hall or "depachika". The food available here is really well presented ranging from seafood to cakes, sweets and pastries, plus readymade food which is a great option for an easy meal if you don't want to head out to a restaurant and just want to get something to take back to your hotel.

We did this on our first night in Tokyo after a very long flight. There are often free samples on offer too!

TIPS

If you show your Passport, you can receive a *Takashimaya Shopper's Card* which gives you a 5% discount on purchases.

There is a tax refund counter on the 11th floor open 10 am-8 pm (you will need your passport to claim a tax refund.)

Coin lockers are available on the 1st floor.

An overseas shipment service is available on the 7th floor.

Takashimaya Times Square

Address: 5-24-2 Sendagaya, Shibuya, Tokyo.
Hours: 10 am-8 pm daily.
Closest Station: 2 min walk from Shinjuku Station. New South Exit.

Mitsukoshi Department Store

TIP the Ginza store has food halls are located on levels B1 and B2.
Address: 4-6-16 Ginza Chuo-Ku, Tokyo.
Hours: 10:30-8 pm daily.
Closest Station: Ginza Station.

Matsuya Department Store

TIPS the Matsuya Department store in Ginza has a food hall located on level B1. There is also a small park on the roof.

Address: 3-6-1 Ginza Chuo-Ku, Tokyo.
Hours: 10:00-8 pm daily.
Closest Station: Ginza Station.

Aqua City Odaiba

A multi-purpose outlet, Aqua City Odaiba is filled with entertainment, retail stores, and restaurants. Some of the stores include Toys r Us and Disney.

Address: 1-7-1 Daiba, Minato City, Tokyo.
Hours: 11 am to 9 pm daily.
Closest Station: Daiba Station.

Ishetan Department Store

There are several Ishetan department stores in Japan. I particularly like the one in Shinjuku. The two basement floors, B1 and B2 have a wonderful array of food you can purchase and offer free samples (a great way to see if you like local foods which may be different to your own, before you purchase them.) There is also a lovely rooftop garden with seats and lots of greenery.

TIPS

Purchase your lunch from the basement floors then take your food to the rooftop garden to eat.
Address: 3-14-1 Shinjuku Tokyo.
Hours: 10.30 am-8 pm daily.
Nearest Station: Shinjuku Sanchrome Station.
Admission: Free.

Daimaru Department Store

This department store is located next to the JR Tokyo Station.

TIPS

The Daimaru department store has a tax-free and foreign currency exchange counter on the 12th floor. Remember to take your passport if you want to use these services.

There is a food hall on the basement floor and restaurants on the 12th and 13th floor.

Address: 1 Chiyoda1-9-1 Marunouchi. Tokyo.
Hours: 10 am-8 pm. Some of the restaurants on level 12 and 13 have longer hours.
Nearest Station: JR Tokyo Station, Yaesu, North Exit
Admission: Free.

Chapter Ten

Nightlife

As well as bars, clubs and restaurants, there are many other events often happening in Tokyo to explore at night depending upon when you visit. For example, over winter the city lights up with illuminations and evening Christmas markets are held. During cherry blossom season in spring, people hold picnics in the park into the evening when the blossoms are illuminated. There are also sake festivals, beer festivals, live music events, firework displays and the traditional summer festivals.

Many venues stay open until late in the evening making them a perfect time to visit as they are often less crowded, examples include the Sumida Aquarium, Mori Art Museum, Tokyo Tower observatory and Tokyo city view which has a 360-degree observatory on the 52nd floor of the Roppongi Hills Mori Tower building. Open until 10pm the views at sunset are wonderful.

Other options for nighttime activities are taking a sunset dinner or drinks cruise on Tokyo Bay or heading to one of the rooftop bars of the skyscrapers in Ginza for dinner, drinks, and a magnificent view of Tokyo. Karaoke bars are also a fun option and are open until late.

TIPS

With the roads less congested at night, taxis are the quickest and most convenient way of getting around.
Don't get stuck, remember that trains stop running around midnight and don't start again until 5 or 6 a.m.
For late-night pubbing and clubbing, head to Shibuya, Shinjuku or Roppongi
It's a great time to visit popular attractions such as museums and art galleries as they often have late opening hours and are less crowded in the evening.

Pachinko Parlours

If you walk past a brightly coloured building with flashing lights and loud music, filled with rows of machines, the chances are it's a Pachinko gaming parlour.

These venues are for adults only and are a cross between a western style slot machine and pinball game. The Pachinko game uses a small silver ball purchased by the player who drops the ball into the machine with the aim of winning more silver balls.

Although gambling is illegal in Japan the Pachinko parlours are allowed as the "winnings" are given in tokens which are then exchanged for food or goods. (There is however a counter close by that exchanges the tokens for money).

Stepping into a Pachinko Parlour can be a shock to the senses and a little intimidating, with the noise from the machines, flashing lights, smell of stale smoke and lack of conversation (Pachinko is a serious business!) however, they are an interesting place to visit and a part of modern Japanese urban culture.

If you would like to visit one of these popular parlours there are many scattered around the city particularly in the northeast of Shinjuku called Kabuki-cho. Note this is a "red light" area of Tokyo.

Players inside a Pachinko Parlour

Bars

Shinjuku

Tokyo has a thriving nightlife with a wide range of bars and nightclubs to visit, especially in the Shinjuku area of Kabuki- Cho the entertainment district. This area contains many hostess clubs, restaurants, nightclubs, and the infamous love hotels.

The very popular Shinjuku Golden Gai is located in this area and is famous for its large number of small bars. The laneways are packed with tiny bars called Nomi Ya with often only enough seats for a few patrons at a time.
Examples of Nomi Ya bars in this area are.

Bar Plastic an 80's themed bar
Bar Bali a tropical themed bar
Bar Kodoji housing a collection of rare Japanese photographs.

The bright red archway signifies the entrance to the entertainment district in Shinjuku.

Entrance to the Kabuki-Cho entertainment district

Shibuya

Shibuya is one of the quieter nightlife areas of Tokyo. If you are in Shibuya in the evening, Nonbei-Yokocho (drunkard's Alley) is an older area filled with tiny micro bars and restaurants worth exploring.

Roppongi

Packed with bars and clubs makes Roppongi a very popular nightlife district which can get very busy on the weekends. Filled with everything from upmarket jazz venues, western style clubs, and dive bars there is something for everyone.

Whiskey tasting in a Roppongi bar

Ginza

An upscale business district and high fashion shopping destination during the day, Ginza transforms into one of Tokyo's top entertainment districts.

Fine dining restaurants, chic bars, and opulent nightclubs can be found in this location.

Much of Ginza's nightlife is hidden from view as many bars and restaurants are located on the upper stories of office buildings.

Examples of bars and clubs in this area include:

Cocktail bars *Star Bar* and *Bar High Five*

Artsty bars *300 Bar* and *Suki Bar*

Luxury nightclub *Genius*

Ebisu

Another area worth visiting for nightlife is the trendy, lively district of Ebisu. Full of bars and restaurants it's a great place to try one of the many Izakaya (Gastro pub) experiences.

Examples of bars in th is area are:

Trench

and *Tram*

Ikebukuro

If you are looking for an intimate craft beer experience, try *Two fingers Bar*

Live music

Tokyo has an eclectic music scene, with a healthy mix of major acts and underground scenes.
Shibuya is home to a large concentration of "live houses," with venues such as Club Quattro and O-Nest.

If you like Jazz, you can find jazz clubs playing live music throughout Tokyo. Two examples are:

Blue Note Tokyo in the Aoyama district. Live Jazz shows and meals are available. Catch the Hanzomon line from Omote sands station to Aoyama station then transfer to the Oedo line and get off at Roppongi.

Bar Maduro live jazz venue in Rappongi Hills serving whiskey, rum, and champagne cocktails.

To find out which acts are playing and where to see them the Website Metropolis (helpfully in English) is a great source of information.
https://metropolisjapan.com/culture/music

Nightclubs

Tokyo is full of top-quality dance venues which are open until the early hours of the morning.
You will need to show identification to enter the clubs.

Some examples of Tokyo nightclubs include:

Genius is located in Ginza for those wanting a luxury nightclub experience.

Zouk Ginza's largest nightclub is located in the basement of the Granbell Square and hotel. With state-of-the-art lighting and sound the mothership located above the dance floor emits laser beams and flashing lights. A VIP seating section is available above the dance floor for a fee if you need a place to rest between songs.

The Mothership at Zouk nightclub

Sound Museum Vision located in Shibuya this subterranean venue is spread over 4 floors featuring themed rooms.

Womb This three-story nightclub located in Shibuya is open nightly with a different theme and music style each night.

Chapter Eleven

Travelling Further Afield

We have been to many places in Japan besides Tokyo, and if you have the time on your trip, these are some of my recommendations to visit.

Arashiyama Sagano Bamboo Grove

Arashiyama Bamboo Grove

Although a little out of the way this bamboo grove is an interesting sight to see. The bamboo stretches high above, behind and in front of you in a seemingly endless maze as you wander its paths. It's a great place to take photographs. Located at the foot of the "Storm"mountains,
Arashiyama can be reached by bus or train from Kyoto Station. The grove is open 24/7 and is free to enter.

TIPS

Visit early or at sunset to beat the crowds.

There is a bus from the Saga Arashiyama Station, to the grove or you can walk in approx. 15 mins.

The town of Arashiyama has many shops and eateries to visit as well as traditional Ryokan if you want to stay overnight or longer.

If you are looking for other things to do in the area there is a scenic train (Sango scenic train) available from the Saga-Torokko station which travels along the Honzu river and gorge.

There is also the Iwatayama Monkey Park where you can feed Japanese Macaque Monkeys fruit and nuts. Cost 550yen open 9-4pm

Several temples are available to visit in the area including the World heritage Tenryuji Temple which looks lovely in autumn and spring.

Studio Ghibli Theme Park

Fans of the popular Studio Ghibli films will enjoy visiting the new theme park representing the worlds of Studio Ghibli. The park is situated in the Expo Achi Commemorative Park in Nagakute city near Nagoya, three hours by train from Tokyo.
The park will be divided into five sections each representing the different films made by Ghibli and include a replica sky garden and robot from Laputas Castle in the sky, a 5 meter high Wooden Totoro, small cinema, shops and a restaurant.
The five areas are the Hill of youth, Ghibli's warehouse, Mononoke's Village,Valley of the witches and Dondoko forrest.

Robot from Laputa Castle in the Sky

TIPS

Each area has timed entry.

Each area has a separate entry fee. You can visit one or more areas.

Tickets need to be purchased well in advance through JTB travel.

https://ghibli-park.jp/

Matsumoto castle

Matsumoto castle is the oldest five story wooden castle in Japan and is a national treasure. It is one of the most beautiful castles in Japan and is made entirely from wood. Matsumoto castle can be reached by train from Shinjuku Station in Tokyo.

Matsumoto Castle and moat

Cost 700 yen for adults, 300 yen for high school students, primary age and under are free.

Opening hours 8.30-4.30pm

TIPS

Avoid visiting during golden week and Obon as the site gets very crowded.

Shoes need to be removed when inside the castle. Shoe bags will be provided at the entrance for you to carry your shoes.

The staircase is narrow and steep so watch your step.

Between 9-4pm there are Princesses and Samurai characters available at the front of the castle to take pictures with you. Look for the "Hospitality Team" banner to find them.

Nara

Nara houses the Buddhist Todai-Ji Temple which is listed as a UNESCO World Heritage Site. There is a 15-meter-high bronze Buddha within the temple, and 1000 wild deer freely roam the temple grounds.

Deer treats can be purchased for 150yen.

The Todai-Ji Temple and gardens can be reached by train from the Nara Kintetsu Station.

Wild Deer

Nearby Mount Yoshiro is a famous cherry blossom viewing site in late March early April when the mountain is covered in Sakura (cherry blossoms)

Hiroshima Peace Park

Hiroshima became famous after being destroyed by an atomic bomb during World War 2. The Japanese have since built a Peace Memorial Park in the centre of Hiroshima as a memorial and symbol of peace. The Genbaku Dome, one of the only buildings left standing after the bomb exploded, can still be seen.

The 1000 paper origami cranes from the story of *Sadako and the thousand paper cranes* are also on display in the peace park.

Genbaku Dome Hiroshima

TIP

The museum displays inside can be quite graphic and confronting and may not be suitable for children.

Hiroshima castle (rebuilt) and the Shukkeien Gardens are both nearby.

Miyajima Island

We found Miyajima Island a wonderful place to stay for a few days and a nice relief from the hustle and bustle of the big cities. There are walking areas around the island with forest, red vermillion bridges, streams, and freely roaming deer to experience.

The island is considered to be holy and contains the Shinto Itsukushima Temple, a World Heritage Site. The bright red Torri gate is enormous.

To reach Miyajima Island you take the ferry from Hiroshima Park (free if you have a JR pass).

Miyajima Island

Takayama

Takayama is a wonderful little town to visit if you want to see what Japan looked like in the past. We stayed in a Ryokan (Japanese inn) here and had the interesting experience of sleeping on futons laid out on tatami mats.

There are many interesting temples, museums, and shrines to visit in this town and the popular anime series Hyouka is set in Takayama.

While in Takayama try their specialty, *Hida Beef.* Takayama is best reached from Nagoya by train.

Takayama

Osaka

Osaka is the third-largest city in Japan and has many interesting things to see, such as Dontonbori which looks like a futuristic scene from the movie Blade Runner or Black Rain. Universal Studios, which features Harry Potter World, is also located in Osaka and a huge hit with our kids.

Dontomburi at night

Universal Studios Osaka.
The Wizarding World of Harry Potter.

For anyone who loved the Harry Potter books and movies, The Wizarding World of Harry Potter located within Universal Studios Osaka is a real must. There is the Hogwarts Castle to explore, several rides including the wonderful *Harry Potter and the Forbidden Journey* and *Flight of the Hippogriff*. You can also wander through Hogsmeade Village where you will find Ollivander's Wand shop where you can purchase the wooden wands of each character. Honeyduke's for sweets and treats. The Three Broomsticks Tavern for non-alcoholic Butterbeer or Butterbeer ice-cream!

We had a fantastic day here and would love to go again. As Harry Potter World is part of Universal Studios, as soon as you have finished exploring here, you can go on to explore the rest of the park and enjoy the other rides.

The Hogwarts Express

https://www.usj.co.jp/e/attraction/att_detail/the-wizarding-world-of-harry-potter.html

TIPS as this part of Universal Studios is extremely popular; when purchasing your tickets, you will be given a timed entry ticket.

Even though there is a lot to see, head to the rides first as they often have long queues.

Tickets can be purchased online in advance.
https://www.usj.co.jp/e/ticket/

Fushimi Inari-Taisha

Fushimi-Inari-Taisha is a huge area filled with 40'000 large, bright Vermillion red Torii Gates winding up the hillside. You can walk all the way to the top, although it is quite a trek. If you do venture to the top, there are miniature shrines filled with stone carvings of sacred foxes and wonderful views into the valley below.

At the base of the torii gates is a local market filled with interesting food stalls selling Dango, Mochi and Taiyaki. *(see the section of Japanese sweets for more information on these treats).*

Fushimi Inari can be reached by train from Kyoto or Osaka as a day trip.

Foxes guarding a shrine in Fushimi Inari Taisha

Kyoto

Kyoto is full of temples, palaces, gardens, and history. There are many things to see in Kyoto, and we easily spent a week here. It was April when we visited, and we were very lucky to see the beautiful cherry trees in blossom. The Golden Temple (Kinkaku-Ji), Silver Temple (Ginkaku-Ji) and Philosopher's walk are all popular sites to see, especially during cherry blossom season. You might even spot a Geisha walking the streets of Gion, just remember to be respectful and ask permission if you want to take a photograph.

Philosopher's Walk Kyoto

Nagano and Sapporo

Nagano and Sapporo are the perfect places to ski and great places to visit in winter if you like snow. A Snow Festival is held in Sapporo each year in early February and features spectacular snow and ice sculptures some 25 meters high!

More information on the festival can be found on their website.

www.snowfes.com/english/

Ice sculptures at the Sapporo Snow Festival

Shiga Kogen

The 1998 Nagoya winter Olympics were held in the Shiga Kogen area, and it is a good place to visit if you want ski slopes that are less crowded than many of the other sites.
Located in the town of Yamanouchi in the Nagano prefecture, Shiga Kogen is close to the town of Shiba Onsen and the Jigokudani Yaen Koen snow monkeys.

If visiting in spring, summer, or autumn, the area also offers good hiking trails. For more information.

https://www.snowmonkeyresorts.com/smr/shiga-kogen/joshinetsu-kogen-national-park/

To get there from Tokyo take a 90-minute Shinkansen bullet train to Nagoya, then local direct bus to Shiga Kogen

Beautiful Shiga Kogen

Shiba Onsen

Shibu Onsen is a lovely spa town situated at the base of Shiga Kogen and features numerous onsens (bath houses) to visit. The traditional character of the town with its quaint laneways and old buildings gives it a real charm. You can collect ink stamps from each onsen on a souvenir cloth to take home with you.

Visiting the onsens is a lovely way to spend the afternoon after a day of skiing, snowboarding, hiking, or exploring.

To reach Shibu Onsen catch the Shinkansen bullet train from Tokyo to Nagoya, then local train to Shiga Kogen.

https://www.snowmonkeyresorts.com/activities/shibu-onsen-9-onsen-visit/

Accommodation at Shibu Onsen

Jigokudani Yaen Koen (Snow Monkey Park)

Located close to Shiga Kogen, the Jigokudani Yaen Koe or Snow Monkey Park, is home to around 200 Japanese Macqaue monkys who love to spend their time bathing and grooming in the hot springs.

These cute animals are a delight to watch and photograph, however give them a little space when watching so as not to disturb them.

Many hotels in the area offer shuttle buses to the area and then there is a 1.6km hike to the snow monkeys.

https://www.snowmonkeyresorts.com/smr/snowmonkeypark/snow-monkey-park-information/

Snow monkeys grooming each other.

Chapter Twelve

Other useful information

Useful phrases

Hello	Kon-ni-chi-wa
Goodbye	sa-yo-na-ra
Yes	hai
No	i-e
Please	ku-da-sai

Thank you	a-ri-ga-to
I don't understand	wa-ka-ri-ma-sen
Do you speak English?	E-go ga ha-na-se-mas ka
How much is it?	I-ku-ra des ka
Where are the toilets?	toy-re wa do-ko des ka
I'm lost	ma-yoy-mash-ta
Call a doctor	i-sha o yon-de
Where's the Station?	E-ki wa do-ko des ka
When's the next bus?	Tsu-gi no bas wa nan-ji des ka
My name is......	wa-ta-shi no na-ma-e wa ....des
What is your name?	o-na-ma-e wa nan des-ka
Men	otoko
Women	onna

Children	Komodo-tachi
Do you take credit cards?	Ku-re-jitto kado hara-e-mass ka

Food

Please bring the bill	o-kan-jo o ku-da-sai
Do you have vegetarian	bejitarian ga haitemasu ka
Do you have fish?	Osakana ga haitemasu ka
Do you have meat?	Oniku ga haitemasu ka
I'd like the menu	me-nyu o o-ne-gai shi-mas
Spicy	spai-shi
Fork	fo-ku
Spoon	spun
Rice	go-han
Noodles	men

Sugar	sa-to
Milk	mi-ru-ku
Water	mi-zu
Coffee	ko-hi
Tea	ko-cha
Beef	gyu-ni-ku
Chicken	to-ri ni-ku
Pork	bu-ta-ni-ku
Eel	u-na-gi
Fish	sa-ka-na
Egg	ta-ma-go
Beer	bi-ru
Red wine	a-ka wain
White wine	shi-ro wain

Numbers

One	i-chi
Two	ni
Three	san
Four	shi/yon
Five	go
Six	ro-ku
Seven	shi-chi
Eight	ha-chi
Nine	ku
Ten	ju
Eleven	ju-ichi
Twenty	ni-ju-ichi
Thirty	san-ju

Forty	yon-ju
One hundred	hyaku
One thousand	sen

Visas and customs

If you are from Australia or New Zealand and are planning on holidaying in Japan for up to 90 days, you will not need a visa as these countries have *Reciprocal Visa Exemption Arrangements*. At immigration, Australian and New Zealand passport holders will be issued with a "Temporary Visitor" entry status stamp.

If you are from another country, you may need a temporary holiday visa to enter Japan, check with your travel agent or online at **https://www.immigrationworld.com/japan/how-to-apply-for-japan-tourist-visa/**

All travellers will require a valid passport and travellers will be asked to fill out an arrival or landing card before going through emigration.

It is standard procedure to have your fingerprints taken when entering the country.

Duty-free allowances when entering Japan are:
400 cigarettes
3 litres of alcohol
57g of perfume
Gifts to the value of 200,000 yen

Prohibited items include:
Firearms and ammunition
Narcotic drugs and stimulants

Codeine
Pornographic material
Animal and plant products may be subject to quarantine.

For more information visit

http://www.customs.go.jp/english/summary/passenger

Information Centres

Tokyo

Tokyo Information Centre, 1st floor. Shin-Tokyo building.

3-3-1 Marunouchi, Chiyoda-Ku, Tokyo.

Open daily 9 am – 5 pm.

Narita Airport

Narita International Airport, Tokyo, Arrival floor, Passenger terminal 2.

Open daily 9 am – 8 pm.

Osaka

Osaka Information Centre, 3rd floor JR Shin-Osaka Station.

5-16-1 Nishinakajima, Yodogawa-Ku Osaka.

Open daily 7 am – 8.30 pm.

Kansai International Airport

Arrival floor, Passenger Terminal Building, Kansai.

Open daily 8.30 am – 8.30 pm.

Kyoto

Kyoto Tourist Information Centre, 2nd floor, Kyoto Station.

Shiokoji-saguru, Kamasuma-dori, Shimogyo-Ku.

Kyoto City.

Open daily 8.30 am–7 pm.

Hiroshima

Hiroshima City Tourist Information Centre, 1st floor,
South Exit, of JR Hiroshima Station.
2-37 Matsubara-cho, Minami-Ku, Hiroshima City.
Open daily 9 am – 5.30 pm.

Sapporo

Hokkaido -Sapporo Tourist Information Centre, JR Sapporo Station,
West Concourse N6, W4, Kita-Ku, Sapporo City.
Open daily 8.30 am – 8 pm.

Embassies in Tokyo

Australia

2-1-14 Mita, Minato-Ku Tokyo 108-831
Telephone 03-5232-4111
www.australia.or.jp

New Zealand

20-40 Kamiya-cho, Shibuya-Ku Tokyo 150-0047
Telephone 03-3467-2271
www.nzembassy.com/japan

United States of America

1-10-5 Akasaka, Minato-Ku Tokyo 107-8420
Telephone 03-3221-5000
www.japan.usaembassy.gov

United Kingdom

1 Ichiban-cho, Chiyoda-Ku Tokyo 102-8381
Telephone 03-5211-1100
www.ukinjapan.fco.gov.uk

Canada

7-3-38 Akasaka, Minato-Ku Tokyo 107-8420

Telephone 03-5412-6200

www.canadainternational.gc.ca/japan-japon

Electricity

The Japanese electric current is 100 volts, 50Hz. In Osaka and Kyoto and other areas of western Japan, the current used is 100 volts, 60Hz.

TIPS

Many hotels provide adapters on request; however, I always bring an adapter from home to charge my mobile phone and camera. Electronics stores such as Bic Camera and Yodobashi Camera sell adapters if you require one.

If you are unsure about which electrical current your country uses, you can go to the website World Standards.

https://www.worldstandards.eu/electricity/plug-voltage-by-country/

Another thing to consider is the type of plug your electrical appliances and devices use such as camera chargers and hairdryers.

For example, Australia uses a three-pronged plug that contains an earth. Japan uses the two flat prongs plug which is the same plug as Canada and North America.

Examples of the different plugs used are shown on this website by World Standards.

https://www.worldstandards.eu/electricity/spread-plug-types-map/#location

Telephones and internet

Mobile Phones

On our first few visits to Japan, it was not possible to use international mobile phones due to differing technologies. Nowadays, it is possible and mobile phone service providers offer international roaming services so you can use your own mobile phone without changing your SIM card. However, you may wish to speak to your provider before you leave home to find out about costs, plans, and any hidden charges. Some phone companies offer travel packages for a set amount each day, and these can be quite convenient. Note that some older style mobile phones may not work in Japan.

Other options include renting a mobile and/or purchasing a Japanese SIM card. SIM cards are available at the airport and retailers such as Bic camera. Your phone must be unlocked to utilize SIM cards.

Further information on mobile phones is provided on the website:

https://www.japan-guide.com/e/e2223.html

Internet

An alternative to using your own data which can be expensive is to rent a mobile personal Wi-Fi or pocket Wi-Fi to which you can connect your phone wirelessly. This is a small device you carry with you on your pocket or bag and connect several devices. We have used this method several times previously and found it very useful for accessing google maps!

TIP. Most cafes, restaurants, hotels, and public areas such as train stations and department stores offer free Wi-Fi which is very useful.

Etiquette

Etiquette is important in Japan, although foreigners are usually forgiven for not knowing the "rules".
Some points of etiquette to be aware of are:

The traditional greeting is a bow; however, foreigners are rarely expected to bow.

When entering a shrine or temple, leave your shoes at the entrance or carry them with you.

Blowing your nose in public is seen as distasteful. You may see people wearing face masks in public to stop infecting others or catching a virus themselves.

Eating while walking is frowned upon. Find a park bench to sit on or take your food back to your hotel.

Do not place chopsticks upright in a bowl of rice or noodles as this is seen as a symbol of death and funerals. Place them by the side of your plate/bowl.

Do not spear your food with your chopsticks.

Talking loudly, especially on your phone, is seen as bad manners.

When waiting for the train or in a store, people line up quietly and don't complain about how long it is taking.

Stand on the right side of escalators and if in a group stand single file so as not to block the left-hand side. Commuters use the left side to walk up or down the escalator when in a hurry.

Health and safety

Toilets

Japanese toilets range from highly sophisticated machines with a multitude of buttons to very basic squat toilets. If using squat toilets, face the end with the hood.

Using one of the hi-tech toilets for the first time can be a little daunting, especially for smaller children (and even adults!), and they may need assistance. Many toilets have self-opening and closing lids, heated seats (both of which I wished we had at home!) and numerous buttons for playing music or water sounds, hot air drying and bidet.

TIP. Toilet paper or hand towels may not always be provided, so I always carry tissues in my handbag. (When wandering the main streets of Tokyo, you will often see people handing out packs of tissues for free, it is a good idea to take a pack of these if offered to you and carry them in your handbag/backpack for just this reason).

Earthquakes/typhoons

Each year Japan experiences more than 1000 earthquakes, and typhoons cause flooding, landslides, and wind damage during the typhoon season of June to October.

The tall city buildings now have mechanisms to absorb the motion of an earthquake, lessening destruction and damage. If caught in an earthquake, the Japanese Meteorological Agency recommends staying indoors and sheltering under a doorway or something sturdy like a desk or table. If you are in the streets, try to find protection from glass and other objects that may fall from surrounding buildings.

Further information can be found on the Japanese MeteorologicalAgencywebsite.

http://www.jma.go.jp/en/quake/

Medical facilities

Medical facilities in Japan are good, although expensive. I always take travel insurance with me when travelling, just in case anyone in our family becomes sick or injured.

Pharmacies are a useful place to go if you are requiring general advice on minor problems.

Larger hotels often have a doctor on call or can help you contact one if needed.

The Japan help-line can be contacted for help with emergency assistance. The call is toll-free, and available 24-hours ph. 0570 000 911

The Tokyo Metropolitan Health and Medical Information Centre for help finding English speaking clinics and hospitals is available from 9 am to 8 pm 03-5285-8181 and in Osaka: 06-4395-0555

Drinking water

Tap water is safe to drink, and bottled water is available in supermarkets and convenience stores. Still water is *mizu,* and sparkling water/mineral water is *mineraru uota.*

Prescription Medication

If you take prescription medication, you may need to see your doctor to ensure that you have enough for your entire trip, plus a little extra in case of delays. Leave your medication in its original packaging and carry a letter from your doctor stating your dose and that it's for personal use. I always carry any medications in my hand luggage, (as long as it complies with airline restrictions on what you can carry onboard such as liquid allowances) just in case my checked baggage goes missing.

It is also important to note that some medications that are available in Australia and overseas, may be classified as restricted in Japan. For example, codeine and any medication containing it, is restricted. Your doctor or pharmacist will be able to advise you if your medication contains codeine if you are unsure.

Western brands of pharmaceutical products are available at some pharmacies such as the *American Pharmacy* in Tokyo; however, prices will be higher than you are used to at home.

TIP Something to be aware of, when I was shopping for head cold medication, I found some Japanese products contained ginseng and caffeine. So, it is always wise to ask the pharmacist about the ingredients of a product if you are unsure or plan on giving the product to any members of your family who may be caffeine sensitive.

National holidays

January 1st New Year's Day

January 15th Coming of Age Day

February 11th National Foundation Day

April 29th Greenery Day

May 3rd Constitutional Memorial Day

May 4th national People's Day

September 15th Respect for the Aged Day

October 10th Sports Day

November 3rd Culture Day

November 23rd Labour Thanksgiving Day

December 23rd Emperor's Birthday

Golden week April 29th to May 5th

Festivals and Events

Japan has many festivals, and if you happen to be holidaying when one occurs, you are in for a wonderful display of sights and sounds.

Some of the main festivals include:
Sapporo Snow Festival or Yuki Matsuri is held in early February (the exact date changes depending on the year). The festival lasts a week and includes an international snow sculpture contest, ice slides and mazes for the kids. There is also food and drink for sale. www.snowfes.com/english

Cherry Blossom Viewing or Hanami usually between March and April; however, their blossoming time can be very unpredictable! There are numerous parks to see the pink and white blossoms including Ueno Park and the Imperial Palace Gardens in Tokyo. Also, the Osaka Castle Park, Osaka Zoheikyoku (Osaka mint) and Ryokuchi-koen Park in Osaka.
Plus, Maruyama Park, Okazaki Canal and Tetsugaku No Michi (The Philosopher's Path) in Kyoto.
We were lucky enough to see the blossoms blooming along the Philosophers path when we visited Japan in April; however, they only lasted a week so it can be pure luck to be in the right place at the right time.

Takayama Spring Festival is held on the 14th and 15th April. The festival consists of a dozen decorated floats (yatai) being lit with lanterns and paraded through the town accompanied by sacred music.

Sanja Matsuri Festival is held in Tokyo for three days every May. Parades of people carrying portable shrines fill the streets of Asakusa. There are traditional drummers, food stalls and thousands of onlookers.

Gion Matsuri held in Kyoto.
This is Kyoto's biggest festival and lasts the entire month of July. The main events are held from the 14th to 17th July with many areas of the city shut off to cars. A parade of elaborate floats carrying musicians and dancers is held on the 17th of July.

Tenjin Matsuri in Osaka
This festival is held on the 24th and 25th July at Tenman-gu Shrine and throughout the city. There are puppet shows, musical performances and two parades of 3000 people and decorative boats. The festival ends with a fireworks display.

Fuji Rock Festival
This is Japan's biggest music festival and is held for three days in late July. Both big name and smaller acts play at this popular event. https://en.fujirockfestival.com/

Other Events

O-Bon (Festival of the dead) is held for three days in mid-August to honour the dead. Offerings are made, and paper lanterns are floated down rivers or lakes to help guide spirits on their journey.

Anime Japan Exhibition held in Tokyo at *Tokyo Big Site* in late March. https://anime-japan.jp/en/

Tokyo Game Show (TGS) this huge computer game expo is held at the Makuhari Messe in Tokyo during September. https://expo.nikkeibp.co.jp/tgs/2019/en/

Sumida-gawa Fireworks in Tokyo This spectacular fireworks display is held every year on the last Saturday in July in Asakusa. Over 20,000 fireworks are exploded during this summer event.

Peace memorial Ceremony held on the 6th of August each year in Hiroshima for victims of the WW2 atomic bombing of the city. Thousands of paper lanterns are floated down the river in remembrance of the victims.

Opening Hours

Post Offices: 9am – 5pm Monday to Friday.
Banks: 9am – 3pm Monday to Friday.
Department Stores: 10am – 8pm Daily.
Museums: 9am – 5pm daily except Mondays (closed).
Restaurants: 11am - 2pm and 6pm - 11pm, Cafes generally open earlier.
Bars: 7pm until late.

Useful telephone numbers

Police emergency: 110

Police general enquiries: 03-3503-8414

Fire and Ambulance: 119

Japan help-line: (Toll free, 24-hour emergency assistance. Multilingual).
0120-461-997

Tokyo Metropolitan Health and Medical Information Centre:
(for help finding English speaking clinics and hospitals)
9am-8pm 03-5285-8181
Osaka: 06-4395-0555

Photo Credits

All the text and images are copyright by Suzanne Lowe except for

Edo Tokyo Map p.39. www.edo-tokyo-museum.or.jp
Disneyland Map p.45 www.tokyodisneyresort.jp
National Museum of Emerging Science and Innovation p.78 www.miraikan.jst.go.jp
Samurai Museum p.107 www.samurimuseaum.jp
Studio Ghibli Map p.121 www.ghiblimuseum.jp
Moiri Digital Art Museum p.151 www.planets.teamlabart/tokyo/
Ueno Park Map p.153 www.japanguide.com
Bed and Book photograph p.162 www.bookandbedtokyo.com
Map of Around Sky Tree p. 169 www.tokyoskytree.jp
Sapporo Snow Festival photograph p.199 www.snowfes.com
Hamster photograph p.210 www.harinezumi-cafe.com/en/mogumogu

Thank you to Tahlia Lowe for her photographs.

Website credits

https://www.jsf.or.jp/en/

https://www.tokyo-dome.co.jp/

https://www.edo-tokyo-museum.or.jp/en/p-exhibition/

www.sankan.kunaicho.go.jp/

https://www.tokyodisneyresort.jp/

https://www.tokyotower.co.jp/

https://www.fujitv.com/visit_fujitv/

https://www.miraikan.jst.go.jp/

https://www.megaweb.gr.jp/

https://www.planets.teamlab.art/tokyo/

https://www.cupnoodles-museum.jp/

https://sunshinecity.jp/

www.skycircus.jp/

https://www.tokyo-zoo.net/

https://www.kahaku.go.jp/

http://www.sensojitemple.com

http://www.tokyo-skytree.jp/

https://en.puroland.jp/

https://www.samuraimuseum.jp/

http://www.yokoso.metro.tokyo.jp/

http://www.fujiq.jp/

http://www.ghibli-museum.jp/

http://www.yomiuriland.com/

https://onepiecetower.tokyo/

https://www.tnm.jp/

https://www.tobikan.jp/

http://www.bandainamco-am.co.jp

www.animate.co.jp/

http://www.akb48cafeshops.com/akihabara/

http://www.customs.go.jp/

https://www.worldstandards.eu/electricity/

https://www.japan-guide.com

www.snowfes.com/

ABOUT THE AUTHOR

Author Suzanne Lowe

Suzanne was born in Perth Western Australia and as a young adult grew up in the small country town of Tom Price situated in the outback of Western Australia.

Having an adventurous spirit, Suzanne has had the opportunity to experience many exciting adventures including swimming with Whale Sharks on Ningaloo Reef in Australia, climbing to Mt

Everest base camp, descending into one of the pyramids at Giza in Egypt, flying in a hot air balloon over the Valley of the Kings, parachuting from a plane at 12000 feet in York, standing on the edge of an active volcano on Tanna Island in Vanuatu, getting up close with Emperor penguins in Antarctica, and sitting with snow monkeys in the hot springs of Yamanouchi, Japan!

She is a member of the International Travel Writer's Alliance, Society of Children's Book Writers and Illustrators, Australian Society of Authors, and the Australian Science Fiction Society.

In 2024 Suzanne produced the Australian feature film *The Canary* with Salt and Honey Productions and Silvergum Creative.

Suzanne's published works

Travel to Tokyo. Everything you need to know about holidaying in Tokyo.

Travel to Tokyo with Kids. A guide to traveling with your family in Japan.

Seventeen, book one of the *Seventeen Series.* A YA dystopian adventure story set in outback Western Australia. *2018 Winner of the New Apple E-book award in YA horror and Sci-Fi. 2020 Bronze medal winner in literature, Readers' Favorite awards.*

Rage, book two of the *Seventeen Series.* A YA dystopian adventure story set in outback Western Australia.

Divided, book three of the Seventeen Series. *Finalist in the 2024 Book Excellence Awards.*

The Pirate Princess and the Golden Locket, a pirate adventure story for middle-grade children. *2019 Bronze medal winner in children's literature, Readers' Favorite international award. 2020 Book Excellence Award in Pre-Teen Literature.*

The Pirate Princess and the Sirens' Song. Book two of the Pirate Princess Series. *2021 Book Excellence Award in Pre-Teen Literature. 2021 Honourable mention Readers' Favorite awards.*

Prepping your Family for an Emergency. A guide for staying safe during an emergency.

You can connect with Suzanne at

www.suzanneloweauthor.com

Twitter: @suzanne_lowe_

Instagram: www.instagram.com/suzannelowe.author/

Facebook: www.facebook.com/suzanneloweauthor/

Seventeen

Book one in the Seventeen Series

Winner of the New Apple YA horror/Sci-Fi award
Science fiction in the Australian outback

Imagine a world where everything you grew up with is gone. No adults, no internet, no rules. Could you survive?
When the KV17 virus kills everyone above the age of seventeen, life becomes a battle of survival for the children left behind. Seeking to escape the escalating violence in the city, two sisters, Lexi and Hadley flee to the Australian outback. Finding sanctuary in the small town of Jasper's

Bay, they soon realise it is far from safe, as a gang of lawless teenagers terrorise the town.

Caught in a bitter feud leading to betrayal, deceit and murder, the girls must quickly uncover who their enemies are, and who they can trust. In a world drastically changed from everything they once knew; can the sisters and children of Jasper's Bay learn to adapt? Can they maintain control of their town, and protect it from those who would destroy it?

https://www.amazon.com/stores/Suzanne-Lowe/author/B01N6O6U52

Travel to Tokyo with kids

A parent's guide for a fun family holiday.

Planning a family holiday to Japan?
Travel to Tokyo with kids will help you make your holiday less stressful.
Talking robots, cartoon characters, ancient temples, and interesting food, Tokyo is an amazing place to visit, but where should you start?

Most travel guidebooks focus on what to do as an adult. What if you are travelling with children or teenagers.

Travel to Tokyo with kids is written for families wanting to travel together. Full of useful tips and practical advice with sections for younger children, teenagers, and young adults.

https://www.amazon.com.au/stores/Suzanne-Lowe/author/B01N6O6U52

Milton Keynes UK
Ingram Content Group UK Ltd.
UKHW051025220724
445737UK00009B/35

9 780648 904984